Knocking Depression With Food

About the author

Dr. Rajat Trehan is a healthcare professional who believes in the power of nutrition and phytotherapy to heal the body and prevent diseases. With his doctorate and master's degree in clinical nutrition and nutritional sciences and certification in plant-based nutrition, he has treated over 10,000 patients worldwide for degenerative diseases like arthritis, diabetes, liver disorders, and post-COVID complications. Dr. Trehan advocates for a natural approach to healing by looking for solutions in nutrition and diet. He encourages people to prioritize prevention over cure by avoiding junk food and adopting healthy eating habits. He has authored two books and an e-book. He also appears on news channels and magazines to spread awareness about natural healing and healthy eating habits.

Knocking Depression With Food

Dr. Rajat Trehan

Heal Our Body
New Delhi

Published by
Dr. Rajat Trehan
B-1/626, Janak Puri,
New Delhi-110058
India
Phone: +91-11-47506464; 9810361459
Email: contact@drrajattrehan.com
Web: www.drrajattrehan.com

2025
Printed in India

Cataloging in Publication Data--DK
Courtesy: D.K. Agencies (P) Ltd. <docinfo@dkagencies.com>

Trehan, Rajat, author.
Knocking depression with food / Dr. Rajat Trehan.
pages cm
Includes bibliographical references.
ISBN 13: 978-93-5980-522-1 ISBN 10: 93-5980-522-X

1. Depression, Mental--Nutritional aspects--India. 2. Depression, Mental--Treatment--India. 3. Diet therapy--India. I. Title.

LCC RC537.T74 2025 | DDC 616.852706 23

Disclaimer

This book provides information for reference purposes only and does not intend to replace or substitute professional medical advice. The author, the publisher, or any person directly or indirectly contributing to the publication or information disclaims any legal claims, express or implied. The information in this book is not a substitute for expert and professional medical advice. The author, publisher, and contributors assume no responsibility for any loss or damage caused, or allegedly caused, directly or indirectly by the use of the information contained in this book. The author and publisher expressly disclaim any liability incurred from the use or application of the contents of this book.

Preface

Depression is a complex and composite mental health condition that affects millions of people worldwide. It is a condition that can impact a person's emotional, mental, and physical well-being, making it difficult for them to function in their daily lives. Despite the widespread prevalence of depression, the underlying causes and effective treatments for this condition remain unclear and often controversial.

As a phytonutritionist, I have spent years researching the connections between diet, nutrition, and mental health. My passion for this field stems from my personal experiences with depression and the realization that food and lifestyle choices can have a profound impact on our mental health.

This book is the result of my extensive research and experience working with individuals who have struggled with depression. In these pages, I hope to provide readers with a comprehensive understanding of the link between diet and mental health, as well as practical strategies for using food as a powerful tool to manage and prevent depression.

In Part One of this book, I delve into the science behind depression, exploring the various factors that contribute to this condition. From the role of neurotransmitters to the effects of inflammation, I provide readers with a detailed understanding of the complex interplay between our brain and body that can lead to depression.

In Part Two, I explore the power of phytonutrients - the biologically active compounds found in plants - to support mental health. Drawing on the latest research, I explain how certain plant-based foods and supplements can modulate inflammation, enhance neurotransmitter function, and improve overall brain health. I also provide readers with practical tips for incorporating these foods into their diet and making meaningful lifestyle changes to support their mental health.

While nutrition and lifestyle choices can be powerful tools for managing depression, they are not a panacea. Throughout this book, I emphasize the importance of taking a holistic approach to mental health. In addition to dietary changes, I encourage readers to seek out supportive relationships, engage in regular exercise, and practice stress-management techniques to promote mental wellness.

In writing this book, my goal is to empower everyone who is reading this book to take control of their mental health and make informed choices about the food they eat and the lifestyle they lead. While depression can be a difficult and challenging condition, I firmly believe that it is possible to find relief and improve one's quality of life through thoughtful and intentional dietary and lifestyle changes.

Ultimately, this book is about hope – the hope that comes from recognizing the power we have to positively impact our own mental health. Whether you struggle with depression or simply want to optimize your mental wellness, I hope that the information and strategies presented in these pages will serve as a valuable resource on your journey towards better mental health.

In conclusion, I want to acknowledge that depression is a severe condition that requires professional medical intervention. While this book provides readers with valuable information and tools for managing depression, it is not a substitute for seeking out professional care. If you or someone you know is struggling with depression, I urge you to seek out the support of a qualified mental health professional. Together, we can work towards a world where mental health is treated with the same level of care and attention as physical health.

Acknowledgements

Gratitude fills my heart as I extend sincere thanks to the remarkable individuals whose steadfast support and expertise have played an indispensable role in the realization of 'Knocking Depression with Food.'

Mr. Rajan Dhir, whose invaluable advice and insightful discussions on health matters have been a guiding beacon. Our exploration of topics ranging from diet and nutrition to the intricacies of life has truly enriched the essence of this book. The 'agreeing to disagree' concept, exemplified through our discourse, embodies the spirit of nonjudgmental dialogues.

Dr. Rajeev Trehan, my brother and source of unwavering motivation, brings expertise in CVTS at Neotia Getwel Health Care Centre, Siliguri, as a constant source of inspiration.

Dr. Meena Trehan, my sister-in-law, a Senior Consultant in Paediatric Cardiac and Anaesthetist, stands as a steadfast pillar of support.

I extend immense gratitude to my former colleagues, Ms. Kavita Kaindal and Ms. Reena Sharma, and my present colleague, Ms. Bhanupriya, for their invaluable support and assistance throughout this endeavour.

Mr. Parminder Singh Kakria and Mr. Karan Hari, mentors for life, have been unwavering motivators and inspirations on this profound journey.

My uncle, Mr. Sunil Badhwar, and Aunt Renu Badhwar deserve heartfelt thanks for their guidance and care while writing this book.

To my friends, your encouragement has been a driving force behind my work.

A special appreciation goes to Ankita Singh, my dedicated editor, who has been with me from the inception of the book till completion. Her guidance and expertise have transformed my words into a polished work of art.

Last but not the least, my heartfelt appreciation to Shhalaj Mittaal from Shhalaj Publishing House for the constant support, invaluable guidance, and seamless cooperation in bringing this book to broader readers.

I extend my sincere thanks to the readers who have welcomed this book into their world. It has been a privilege to share this work with you, made possible by the remarkable individuals and entities mentioned above.

Warm regards,
Dr. Rajat Trehan

Introduction

Dear Reader,

Depression is a debilitating condition that affects millions of people worldwide. As a phytonutritionist with decades of experience in phyto medicine, I have seen firsthand how this condition can impact the lives of individuals and their families. Depression not only affects one's mood but can also lead to physical health problems and a decreased quality of life.

Through my years of research and practice, I have come to understand the importance of a holistic approach in treating depression. This approach includes not only addressing the biological and psychological aspects of the condition but also considering the role of nutrition and plant-based medicine in supporting the body's natural healing mechanisms.

This book is the result of my passion for helping people overcome depression and regain their health and vitality. I have written it with the hope of providing practical, evidence-based information to those who are struggling with depression or know someone who is.

In this book, I will explore the science behind depression and its relationship to nutrition and plant-based medicine. I will share with you the latest research on the role of specific nutrients and plant compounds in supporting brain function and reducing symptoms of depression.

But this book is not just about science. It is also about my personal journey and the stories of those I have helped over the years. I have seen firsthand how simple changes in diet and lifestyle can have a profound impact on one's mental health.

My goal is to empower you with the knowledge and tools you need to take control of your health and overcome depression. Whether you are struggling with mild symptoms or have been diagnosed with a severe form of depression, this book is for you.

I believe that everyone can benefit from the information in this book, regardless of age or gender. Whether you are a busy professional, a student, a parent, or a retiree, the strategies and tips outlined in these pages can help you achieve better mental and physical health.

I invite you to join me on this journey towards optimal health and well-being. Together, we can take small steps towards making meaningful changes in our lives and the lives of those around us.

Sincerely,
Dr. Rajat Trehan

Contents

1

Depression and Anxiety: What do You Know about Each?

People often use the terms depression and anxiety together. However, they both have entirely different meanings. Anxiety is feeling nervous, unsettled, or stressed. In comparison, depression is a severe condition that gives birth to suicidal and self-harming thoughts. Unfortunately, it often goes undiagnosed until it is in its later stages.

It is essential to have basic knowledge of these terms in order to recognize their signs and symptoms at an initial stage, whether in self or others, for timely diagnosis and early intervention. You can save a life!

Some other conditions associated with these include generalized anxiety disorder, panic disorder, phobias, burnout and stress, and obsessive-compulsive disorder or OCD. Each of these varies in symptoms and intensity, may or may not have triggers, but undoubtedly requires immediate attention for mental and physical well-being.

You may be wondering, how these conditions develop. Simply put traumatic incidents, toxic environments, inability to communicate or suppressed feelings and emotions may be responsible for anxiety and depression. Surprisingly, even nutrition plays a vital role in the development of these conditions. Consuming food with higher nutritional value, better taste and to one's liking naturally results in a better mood, instead of following unhealthy crash diets,

Anxiety

Anxiety may be good or bad. Good anxiety is the one we experience before an interview or facing an audience on the stage for the first time. This kind of anxiety is helpful in increasing confidence and performance. On the other hand, bad anxiety may include severe emotional or physical reactions to certain triggers.

This type may provoke abnormal behaviour and have physical implications—for example, separation anxiety in dogs and humans or flight reaction on sensing certain fearful situations.

Triggers for anxiety are different for every individual. These depend on the person's experiences, thought processes, genetics, development, psychology, environment, and other factors.

Anxiety affects not only the mind but also the body and may exacerbate any ongoing medical condition. Commonly, people experience jitters or butterflies in the stomach, nervousness, excessive sweating, cold, clammy palms, grinding teeth while asleep, restlessness, and sometimes body ache. Some may feel sick and dizzy, while others may defecate more frequently than usual. Don't be surprised if your sex drive changes, too!

Like depression, it may be difficult to diagnose anxiety since people don't realize that they are suffering from a disorder and need help. People often fail to address the condition until it has advanced to a late stage. As a result, its resolution takes time.

Depression

Depression is one of the principal reasons for disability in the world. Whether it is the increasing competition among people or the pressure to perform better in various aspects of life, such as relationships, work, health, wealth, or social status, the reasons for depression are endless. Some may feel lonely, while others may not be getting support in life. Having such emotional issues for infinite reasons may lead to depression.

One must note that depression is not a disease that we can just name, such as diabetes. It is a condition rather challenging to speak about since the person suffering from it may not even know that they are depressed.

Depression may be a condition in which a person may have pent-up emotions and feelings in their hearts that were left unexpressed or disregarded.

Unfortunately, this condition often leads the person to commit suicide. The harsh truth is that the thought of committing suicide may seem the only choice the person is left with. However, that is not true. Help is available if you seek to change things.

To seek help, we must first learn to recognize the signs of depression in ourselves or the people around us, then develop an approachable attitude towards them and seek help. Also, we must not be hesitant when asking for help in dealing with our emotions. It may sound trivial, but in reality, it isn't.

In India, people often find it challenging to approach psychologists or counsellors, thinking that they may be declared to be mad. However, we must understand that seeking counsel only makes our lives better. We must normalize talking about our emotions openly with the people we trust or professionals, as needed. Taking one step forward will bring you closer to success.

Generalized Anxiety Disorder

When life is stressful, it is normal to be anxious from time to time. However, when this anxiety is ongoing, excessive, difficult to control, and becomes a day-to-day thing, it may be considered a generalized anxiety disorder. This disorder is a very broad term and needs further investigation for appropriate treatment.

This condition may affect children, teens or adults. It may occur along with other disorders or alone. It can be managed with counselling, making lifestyle changes, different forms of behavioural therapy, and medications.

PHOBIAS

A phobia is fear of a place, person, situation, or activity. It is an extreme fear that triggers anxiety in an individual and invokes a flight or flight response in an individual.

For example:

- **Acrophobia:** Fear of heights.
- **Ophidiophobia:** Fear of snakes.
- **Cynophobia:** Fear of dogs.
- **Astraphobia:** Fear of storms.
- **Pteromerhanophobia:** Fear of flying.
- **Claustrophobia:** Fear of enclosed spaces.
- **Entomophobia:** Fear of insects.
- **Trypanophobia:** Fear of needles and medical procedures.

People may even be apprehensive of things that do not pose any threat. For example, fear of insects, flying, and even germs! People thus avoid their phobias because confronting them may worsen their condition.

PANIC DISORDER

Panic disorder is the sudden occurrence of panic attacks or bouts of fear. These may or may not have triggers. It often occurs due to traumatic emotional experiences, but it may have other reasons, too.

Some people experience panic attacks so frequently that they may trigger future panic attacks.

BURNOUT AND STRESS

When we constantly stress about a particular situation, it can lead to burnout. This type of prolonged or chronic stress can cause physical and mental exhaustion, negatively impacting our overall well-being. For example, constantly worrying about your finances and working all the time just to earn a few extra bucks without having significant time to relax can lead to burnout. As a result, you will be tired of working and need a break to recuperate.

Experiencing excessive and prolonged stress can lead to physical, emotional, and mental fatigue. This results in reduced efficiency, energy depletion, and increased mental distance from work.

OBSESSIVE COMPULSIVE DISORDER (OCD)

Obsessive-compulsive disorder is a condition in which people feel the need to do certain things repetitively. It warrants the need for people to eliminate unwanted recurring thoughts, sensations or ideas (obsessions) by doing some activity repeatedly (compulsive). These activities affect social interactions and day-to-day life. Some examples include washing hands, keeping belongings in their designated places, aligning objects parallelly, etc.

References

1. https://www.mind.org.uk/information-support/types-of-mental-health-problems/anxiety-and-panic-attacks/anxiety-disorders/
2. https://www.cdc.gov/tobacco/campaign/tips/diseases/depression-anxiety.html
3 https://www.helpguide.org/articles/stress/burnout-prevention-and-recovery.htm

Common Questions on Depression

Depression affects millions of people in the world every year and is becoming one of the primary reasons for suicides, especially among the younger population. The number of affected people is only rising day by day. Indians, as we know it, still frown upon and consider mental health issues a taboo. But this needs to be changed. It requires attention and better acceptance for seeking treatment throughout the world.

Many teenagers, young adults and those in their early forties are increasingly being targets of untreated depression, leading to higher numbers of suicides in the country.

Recognizing that you have depression and taking action towards improving your life are the only steps you can take to prevent such a massive act. If you don't stand up for yourself or your near and dear ones, you cannot bring a change in the society.

Some statistics on people affected by depression and basic answers to the questions that you may have about depression. are being iscussed in this chapter.

Prevalence of Depression in India and the World

General anxiety disorder and other forms of depression annually affect about 280 million people of all ages, accounting for 3.8% of the world's population. The information provided came from the World Health Organization (WHO). They expect the disorder to burden most nations of the world more than other diseases in the next ten years.

Major depressive disorder was considered the third leading cause of disability in 2015. The global prevalence of mood disorders was estimated to be about 5.4%. In contrast, its prevalence across countries, as per the WHO-World Mental Health Survey, ranged between 0.8-9.4%.

Estimates suggest that almost one-third of healthcare patients in India experience symptoms of depression.

Research indicates that women experience depression more frequently than men. The highest prevalence is among teenagers and middle-aged people. It has a gradual onset and can affect you at any point of time.

India falls under the category of the highest prevalence of mental ailments globally, accounting for 3.5-4.7% of people being affected by the disorder.

This is because we have the least awareness and an underdeveloped infrastructure for addressing mental health needs. Also, people here are not so open about dealing with their mental health and consider such people mad.

However, this thinking has changed to some extent in metro cities due to the positive attitude of the youngsters. However, people still need to change their mentality towards mental health concerns.

CAN DEPRESSION BE CURED?

Depression is a disorder that develops gradually, with multiple factors playing a role in its development. It has periods of recovery and remission based on the severity and triggering factors of the attitude of surrounding people.

Determining whether it's curable can be difficult due to its complexity.

This is because dealing with depression can be challenging, and every mind functions and reacts differently. The treatment of depression depends upon the willingness of the individuals to improve their lives. So, the chances of cure are higher in milder cases with early intervention than in severe ones.

Feelings of loneliness and hopelessness, commonly observed in patients with depression, can recur and worsen other associated symptoms even after completing therapy.

For some people, therapy may work in combination with maintenance self-care measures such as yoga, meditation, and other alternative treatments. In contrast, some people may require several years of therapy to achieve the desired results. However, please note that even though symptoms of depression wean off, there is always a risk of relapse.

Symptoms might ease your life to the extent of you returning to your usual routine. But your depressed mood and mindset may still linger. Plus, you should know that depression is episodic in nature. There is always a possibility of another episode occurring in future.

Experts recommend following self-care measures after completion of therapy and also returning for counselling as soon as you feel your symptoms are recurring. The timely intervention will prevent the worsening of symptoms and improve your life.

Research suggests that depression has a high risk of recurrence. However, it doesn't recur for all.

A 2018 research reports one-third of non-clinical participants have more than one episode of depression. At the same time, the clinical samples had more than 75% of people with multiple episodes.

Older research from 2007 reports at least half the participants with depression have more than one episode, and 80% with two episodes have chances of multiple episodes in the future.

This research indicates that depression returns for most people. However, having only one episode doesn't mean you'll never have more. Therapies, self-care and coping techniques help lower the chances of recurrent episodes. More importantly, these strategies help manage future episodes, if any.

CAN DEPRESSION RELAPSE? IF YES, THEN WHAT IS ITS PREVALENCE?

As already discussed, depression can relapse. However, the chances of relapse of depression differ from case to case. Researchers have extensively explored the risks of relapse and methods for preventing or managing it.

They concluded that individuals can manage future episodes of depression by applying the lessons learned during past therapy, regardless of the potential for relapses. Approaching psychologists become much easier the second time, resolving issues faster than before.

While depression is highly treatable for all mental health conditions, dealing with it can be tough. If you have experienced two more episodes, you are likely to take a 70-90% increased risk of future recurrent episodes. In fact, individuals who have had major depressive disorder face a 60% risk of experiencing a relapse.

This disorder has not only personal implications but also public health consequences. The treatment and recurrence question the community's ability to make provisions to find a resolution. Moreover, they must make arrangements to improve infrastructure, facilities and approachability for everyone.

While prevention of recurrence is highly desirable, it is not always possible to recover completely. Parts of our past often haunt us in the future. Experts suggest that individuals should learn alternative therapies to manage their emotions effectively.

Researchers have now begun to identify risk factors that are specific to recurrence, which are often different from risk factors of the first onset of depression.

WHEN DOES DEPRESSION RELAPSE?

Remember that feeling low from time to time is natural for everybody. But when this sadness lingers, it becomes an issue that needs attention. When you take therapy for the first time, you must have identified some cause or triggering factor while speaking to a counsellor.

Psychologists often help determine the root cause of depression. Through talks, they help us understand where our outbursts of emotions stem from and teach methods of overcoming or dealing with those thoughts. When you find yourself in similar situations, it is essential that you gauge your case and take steps accordingly. Avoid ignoring your feelings and thinking that time will heal. It doesn't. It only worsens your condition.

You may be thinking that despite therapy and treatment, why does depression relapse? We have enlisted below some valid reasons to enhance your understanding of this condition:

- Changes in family situations
- Hormonal changes
- Work-related or financial burdens
- Chronic illnesses also put stress on the body and mind.
- Lacking sleep or inability to sleep
- Incomplete treatment of the first depressive episode
- Being unaware of your own triggers can also surface forgotten memories and trigger relapse.
- Negative self-talk or having low self-esteem and lack of confidence also adds to an increased risk of relapse.

To summarise, it is essential to complete the therapy you have started, seek help when needed, and try to improve your quality of life. Suicide or giving up is not the only choice. You can make a difference; it is possible to change your life. All you need to find is the courage within to accept and take all the help you need.

CAN DEPRESSION BE CURED ON ITS OWN?

Depressive symptoms often occur due to triggering events or as an outburst of pent-up emotions. Furthermore, depression is episodic. The condition goes through periods of remission and intensification, which can create the mistaken impression of being cured. However, your reaction to every triggering situation will intensify with time.

Simultaneously, you may be unable to focus on your work, have feelings of shame and guilt, and face difficulties standing up for yourself.

Treating depression becomes increasingly challenging as it is difficult to cure on its own. It needs proper evaluation and healing time. It is essential to be compassionate towards yourself and know that things will be alright one day.

CAN DEPRESSION GO UNNOTICED?

Can depression really go unnoticed? Sounds ridiculous, right? How could you possibly have it and not know it? Well, it's very much possible. Depression is not like diabetes or any other disease that shows clinically evident and bothersome symptoms like frequent urination, thirst, nausea and constipation. Instead, it's a mental health condition that significantly affects how we feel, think and behave in response to various emotional and physical problems.

It is a disorder that causes persistent sadness, mood swings, and a lack of interest in life. It develops symptoms gradually that may seem frequent mood swings occurring around the menses or work-related stress but worsen as the disease progresses. With time, the symptoms become consistent and start affecting the quality of life. Your relationship with family and other social interactions may also become hollow due to depression.

Some people realize there's something wrong with them and seek help immediately. In contrast, some others may still be clueless about what's going on.

People surrounding you might notice and caution you about it. But if that does not happen, the symptoms may sadden you to the extent of feeling worthless, having low self-esteem and also suicidal thoughts. That's when most people consult psychotherapists for treatment.

WHAT DOES DEPRESSION LOOK LIKE?

You wake up in the morning, begin your routine with exercise or a run, return home, cook, clean, get your husband and kids ready for work and school, and then sit all by yourself once they are gone.

And... depression sinks in.

In the evening, you see them again. You smile, laugh, and keep going on with life. However, there's a sense of emptiness, loneliness and low self-worth. The confidence to go out is lost there. That feeling is what depression is. People from different walks of life can apply the above example.

In a nutshell, superficially, people continue to live their lives normally, but inside, they feel hopeless. And, as their depression worsens, doing day-to-day tasks such as bathing, going to work, or studying becomes troublesome. It can be challenging to detect depression in oneself, as individuals experiencing it may not even realize they have it. Some may know they are depressed and get treated, while others may come out of it and have an epiphany later. However, most people may have no clue and continue on the path of self-destruction.

Therefore, it is crucial to know the symptoms of depression, to be able to recognize them in self and others and approach it in a practical and beneficial way. Depression can take hold gradually, without the depressed person realizing that their feelings and thoughts are becoming increasingly dominant in their perspectives of life.

Most people believe that identifying depression is easy. However, this is not true. They think it manifests as persistent sadness that doesn't seem to lift spirits and heal the person. In fact, it has various forms of presentation.

Surprisingly, even while reading this, you may feel that something is not quite right and relate to feelings of constant fatigue and a need to sleep all the time.

Some of you may experience insomnia, forgetfulness and difficulty in enjoying the simple pleasures of life. According to the book *10 Steps to Take Charge of Your Emotional Life by Dr. Eve. A. Wood,* women often say that they're not depressed.

However, it is precisely this indifference that may indicate depression.

The signs of depression can be subtle yet confusing. But remember that depression can affect your social interactions, family relationships, and future generations and can also be life-threatening. In addition, research suggests that the chronic effects of major depression on the brain can lead to relapse in the future.

The American Psychological Association suggests that women are more likely to be depressed and dysthymic (have persistent low-level depression) than men.

Also, the chances of misdiagnosis in women are higher, probably owing to their mood swings and other premenstrual symptoms. Fortunately, improving one's quality of life can treat depression successfully.

WHEN AND HOW DO I KNOW IF I HAD DEPRESSION?

Depression affects different people in different ways. The intensity, symptoms, and reasons are all varied. The response an individual has to an emotional or physical problem depends on multiple factors like their home environment, upbringing, childhood traumas, social interactions, nature of an individual, their perspectives, genes, and a lot of other such things.

Depression can be confusing. No matter how ridiculous it sounds, depression often goes unnoticed and undiagnosed. It causes persistent sadness, mood swings, and a lack of interest in life. Its occurrence is so slow that you may not even be able to distinguish it from other moods. People may perceive you as cranky or sad. On the one hand, your world may seem falling apart, while on the other, you may be laughing out loud when surrounded by people.

Most symptoms of depression are common, but not everyone necessarily experiences the same symptoms. From the outside, you may look normal, but in the inside, everything may be hurting too much. Sadness, disappointment in self, and other such self-directed negative opinions gradually form a part of the routine. In addition, emotional or physical responses may cause immense trauma. As a result, many people with depression cry on trivial matters, make mountains of a mole and take everything that happens too seriously than they usually would.

Although some signs of depression, such as hopelessness and sadness, are obvious, others may be subtle and easily hidden. Below are some signs you need to be aware of indicating depression. If you can relate to any of them or know of someone going through it, you should seek help immediately.

Also note that some symptoms may overlap with other medical issues, too. Resolving these issues might require seeking a professional opinion, as they can be difficult to fix on your own.

Negative Self-Talk

Depressed people often are less hopeful about the outcomes of routine actions. They feel no matter what they do, they will take a turn for the worse. For example, a compulsive urge to have someone accompany you when going for grocery shopping. It's a task that an average individual can do on their own. However, if you are depressed, you may need someone with you at all times.

If someone denies the help that you asked for, it may feel traumatic. Sudden emotions of sadness and loneliness may stir up. At such times, you may just start blabbering to yourself, saying you're not worthy of company. Self-worth may go for a toss, and so does confidence.

Depressed people often have negative self-thoughts. They feel incapable of doing certain tasks and feel unworthy of joy, pride, serenity, hope, love and gratitude.

The negative self-talk becomes a routine, inner dialogue which is damaging and self-critical. Constantly telling yourself that you are not capable and that you do not deserve love, in turn, teaches your subconscious mind the same thing. As a result, you attract such incidents that aggravate your condition. Long-term negative self-talk can impair cognitive function.

Personality Differences

Depression causes a significant change in your personality. It can make you too quiet and withdraw from everyone, yet also angry and irritable. Instead of being just sad and low, some people may express irritability and overt or suppressed anger.

More or so, outgoing people become introverts and wish to be left alone.

- Physical pain and health ailments
- Alcohol, smoking, or substance abuse
- Disinterest in hobbies

- Appetite and changes in body weight
- Sleep disturbances
- Easy fatigue

Conclusion

If you can relate to any of the signs, you may be depressed. However, just experiencing a few symptoms may not be enough to diagnose your condition. And that is because various kinds of mental health disorders have overlapping symptoms.

It is thus essential to get in touch with a professional as soon as you recognize these symptoms. It is possible to help yourself and others. Your one step forward can save a life. Depression is not the end of life. It is fixable and curable with the help of therapy, and you will feel better. Remember that "Change is the only constant in life".

References

1. https://www.medicalnewstoday.com/articles/325513#negative-self-talk
2. https://www.verywellmind.com/depression-coming-back-signs-of-a-relapse-5094675
3. https://www.ncbi.nlm.nih.gov/pmc/articles/PMC4318605/
4. https://www.ncbi.nlm.nih.gov/pmc/articles/PMC6278224/#:~:text=%5B1%5D%20We%20found%20a%20decrease,often%20by%20those%20with%20depression.

IS DEPRESSION HEREDITARY?

Depression is a common mental health condition prevalent across the globe and has affected over 350 million people. Depression definitely has a hereditary risk, but how much genes alone are responsible for causing depression is yet to be figured out.

Suppose a person's parent or sibling has depression. In that case, it does not necessarily mean they will pass it on to the next generation. There is a possible 30% risk in hereditary cases, compared to the 10% risk among ordinary people. For example, if anyone in the immediate family has experienced a depressive phase in their early ages, the risk increases four to five fold in other members of the family.

Interestingly, recurrent depression may carry a higher risk of developing hereditary depression.

To prevent depression from being passed on from one generation to the next, parents can cultivate the correct home environment and practise healthy eating and sleeping habits. These simple steps can build a better foundation for children and their coming generations, reducing the risk of depression.

Genes and Depression

Depression does not arise from a single gene, unlike many disorders such as sickle cell anaemia, diabetes, and Huntington's disease. Instead, it is the result of the complex interplay of genes, environment and biological factors.

Even though families may have a history of such conditions, mental health disorders cannot be inherited from parents per se. The inherited genetic combination only makes you more likely to develop depression. Several other factors, such as the use of substances, a history of trauma, and a toxic family environment, can contribute to the odds.

Depression and Genetics in Twins

Researchers have compared the risk of genetic factors on depression in identical twins who share 100% of their genes and also in unidentical twins having 50% of the same genetic makeup. Therefore, if genes affect the development of depression, identical twins must show a much higher risk of developing depression than others.

Through studies like these, researchers have determined that heritability is about 40% to 50%. It may be even more in cases of severe depression.

DOES THE HERITABILITY OF DEPRESSION AFFECT CHILDREN?

People with depression are often concerned about passing it on to their children. However, it is essential to understand that depression is a multifactorial disorder. Your children carrying that gene makes them more susceptible to the condition than those who don't.

Alternatively, if a child lacks a family history of depression and does not carry the depression gene, exposure to triggers such as trauma may still lead to depression.

References

1. https://www.ncbi.nlm.nih.gov/pmc/articles/PMC6065213/
2. https://psychcentral.com/depression/is-depression-genetic
3. https://med.stanford.edu/depressiongenetics/mddandgenes.html
4. https://psychcentral.com/depression/top-relapse-triggers-for-depression-how-to-prevent-them
5. https://www.verywellmind.com/is-depression-genetic-1067317

Problems Associated with Depression and Anxiety

Depression and anxiety are not the only mental health issues people deal with. There are many depression-associated conditions that people experience, only that they vary in intensity, duration, and symptoms. Only experts can clinically distinguish these conditions based on different approaches to intervention.

Generalized Anxiety Disorder

GAD, or generalized anxiety disorder, is a persistent and excessive worry about usual, day-to-day things. People with GAD tend to exacerbate minor setbacks and anticipate disastrous outcomes of things that apparently have nothing to be concerned about. They show extreme concern about relationships, money, work, health, and other such matters. It is often difficult for them to control their emotions and anxiety. As a result, they overdo things and overthink situations.

PHOBIAS

A phobia is an anxiety disorder triggered by the fear of any object or situation. When facing a particular problem causes anxiety and refrains you from confronting it may indicate having a phobia.

For example, a simple thing such as climbing up a ladder to access a cupboard at a greater height may invoke fear, shivering, denial (to climb the ladder), cold-clammy skin, and profuse sweating. Even though you know it is safe to climb a ladder, you may be terrified to do it. Thinking about the phobic object or situation can even induce anxiety.

But how does fear affect mental health? We just established the response of a fearful individual to anxiety. But, if the answer to this anxiety is out of proportion to the danger, lasts for over six months, and creates a significant impact on routine life, it becomes a phobia.

PANIC DISORDER

Panic disorder is a state in which a specific situation triggers sudden bouts of anxiety. These episodes are sudden and range from mild to severe in intensity. They do not have a particular pattern, but some events might trigger them.

Everyone has a natural response to stressful and dangerous situations in the form of anxiety and panic. But when they occur regularly and increase in severity at times, it is termed a panic disorder.

BURNOUT AND STRESS

According to WHO, chronic workplace stress that remains unmanaged successfully can cause a syndrome known as burnout. It has three dimensions: feelings of energy depletion or exhaustion, increased mental distance from the job, feelings of negativism or cynicism related to the job, and reduced professional efficacy.

In simple words, burnout is mental, physical and emotional exhaustion caused by prolonged work stress. As the stress continues, you lose motivation and interest to work and feel drained. All the goals and ambitions you once had for yourself concerning your career, go for a toss.

Burnout reduces productivity and drains energy. It makes you feel helpless, cynical, hopeless and resentful. As a result, you feel like you have done everything and have nothing more to give.

Every aspect of your life can be affected, including social life, work and home life. Burnout can also lead to long-term changes in the body, making you vulnerable to ailments like cold and flu. It is a gradual process and does not happen overnight.

OBSESSIVE-COMPULSIVE DISORDER (OCD)

Obsessive-compulsive disorder is a condition in which a pattern of unwanted recurring thoughts, sensations or ideas (obsessions) compels the affected person to do some activities repeatedly (compulsive). For example, washing hands, keeping belongings in designated places, aligning objects parallelly, etc. These activities affect social interactions and day-to-day life.

The repetitive actions may or may not disrupt routine life entirely. However, the thoughts of OCD people are persistent and intrusive, with a rigidness in their behaviour. If they do not adhere to their behaviours, it causes them great distress and a fear of dire consequences.

Some people with OCD are aware that their obsessive thoughts are unrealistic, while others think of them as genuine. Despite that, people find it difficult to disengage from their obsessive thoughts or cease their compulsive behaviour.

References

1. https://adaa.org/understanding-anxiety/generalized-anxiety-disorder-gad
2. https://www.mayoclinic.org/diseases-conditions/generalized-anxiety-disorder/symptoms-causes/syc-20360803
3. https://www.helpguide.org/articles/stress/burnout-prevention-and-recovery.htm
4. https://www.who.int/news/item/28-05-2019-burn-out-an-occupational-phenomenon-international-classification-of-diseases#:~:text=%E2%80%9CBurn%2Dout%20is%20a%20syndrome,related%20to%20one's%20job%3B%20and

2

Can Food Treat Depression: Challenges, Benefits, and Therapies

Depressive disorders have become highly common among the people. They have a powerful effect on the quality of life and are heavy on the pocket since most insurance doesn't cover it. The worst part is the associated higher rate of morbidity and mortality.

There are many effective treatments available, including antidepressant medications and psychotherapy. These two are the first line of therapy for ages. They have changed many lives over the years worldwide and continue to do so, even today. However, even though these modalities work for some people, they may not be effective for others. Thus, there's some room for improvement.

Therefore, it becomes critical to discuss the limitations and challenges faced during the treatment of depression and their outcomes to introduce newer approaches towards solution-based therapy.

Although new treatments have developed in the past decades, their efficacy is not up to the mark for treating depression completely. Moreover, it is currently not feasible to predict who is more likely to benefit from which type of intervention. People often try several therapies before figuring out which treatment helps them the most. The underlying mechanisms of how every treatment works need to be understood better. This limited understanding of the boundaries of depression and heterogeneity is then responsible for most of the misunderstandings surrounding it.

Although researchers have conducted numerous studies to gain a better understanding of depression, it is our lack of knowledge that prevents us from treating depression. In the past few decades, researchers have conducted more than 500 randomised trials to examine the effectiveness of antidepressant medications and over 600 trials for gauging the effects of psychotherapies for treating depression. However, only a fraction, say less than 20% and 30%, respectively, have a low-risk basis. As a result, the outcomes seem uncertain.

Even today, major depressive disorder remains the most common yet underdiagnosed and untreated disorder by clinicians in clinical practice. Thus, the statistical power of such trials is insufficient to determine a treatment's effectiveness, making the modality unreliable. In fact, there is still a lot to learn about approaches that actually work in treating depression.

Living with depression can take a toll on the quality of life of the self and those surrounding us. It is a debilitating and life-threatening mental illness that takes over 7,00,000 lives every year, as per the WHO. With proper help, guidance, treatment, support and medications, it is possible to treat depression to a great extent. People can lead a healthy and happy life later. However, relapse is always a threat.

With this, let us discuss specific challenges that cause relapse and make it difficult to treat depression. We will also discuss other factors responsible for causing limitations in treating depression.

Challenges Related to the Treatment of Modalities

The conventional therapies followed by clinicians to treat depression include psychotherapy, prescription medications, self-help options and certain stimulation procedures. The listed treatment options may not always be sufficient for an individual. Owing to diversity in the aetiology of the development of depression, people may need more than just therapy. While some are comfortable pouring their heart out to a stranger, others might prefer numbing their symptoms with medications.

Researches suggest that conventional methods of treating depression have their own limitations. Mental health is not a disease like Covid-19. You take medications, and symptoms just wean off with time. It doesn't work like that for depression. Our mind keeps rewinding and going back to past traumatic memories. We tend to overthink things and feel the pain or sorrow of our past traumas until we become immune to the pain. Relapse can occur anytime after treatment without prior notice, leading to a setback in progress.

First, let's talk about the primary line of treatment, psychotherapy, which has limitations. It is never a quick fix, and it needs time and patience. In addition, people don't find it comforting to pay just to speak about their emotions. However, they only understand its value once they overcome their fears and take control of their feelings.

Secondly, prescription drugs are helpful in numbing anxiety and controlling emotions. Many might be unaware that even though they help with symptoms of depression, they are a temporary fix. These drugs carry their own side effects, too.

Lastly, understand the limitations that self-help strategies pose. These are highly variable and may not be ideal for all cases. Further, they may benefit milder cases but need more structuring when treating moderate to severe forms of depression.

SUDDEN CHANGES IN LIFE

It's a common saying that change is the only constant thing in life. We go through different phases of life to learn what we have come on earth for and will die one day. Sometimes, these sudden changes can be overwhelming and cause a relapse of depressive symptoms. And nobody is immune to sudden changes and events in life."

SUBSTANCE ABUSE

The most challenging aspect of treating depression is when the affected person is addicted to substances, alcohol or smoking.

References

1. https://link.springer.com/article/10.1007/s40263-012-0028-8
2. https://journals.sagepub.com/doi/10.1177/0004867420915279
3. https://www.thelancet.com/journals/lanpsy/article/PIIS2215-0366(20)30036-5/fulltext
4. https://www.verywellmind.com/treatments-for-depression-1065502
5. https://www.depression.org.nz/the-causes/ongoing-challenges/

Benefits, Side-Effects & Limitations Of Conventional Treatment

Clinical depression is a serious condition with long-lasting implications on the life of the affected individual. The symptoms can be devastating, not only emotionally but also physically. With the increasing competitiveness among people, abuse of drugs, alcohol and cigarettes, stress, sedentary lifestyle, and other such reasons, depression can be inescapable. It has thus become one of the most common disorders affecting the world today.

But remember, depression is unlikely to resolve on its own. Neglected and untreated cases, often for months and years, can destroy not only one life but many. Families, friends and other people in your life are also affected by your depression to a great extent.

Treatment of depression is essential, and we should never overlook or give it a backseat. The reason is as the disorder progresses, it deteriorates the quality of our life, gives rise to thoughts of self-harm and suicide, worsens physical health and also affects any ongoing medical conditions such as diabetes, cardiovascular diseases, hormonal imbalances, etc. Moreover, it can be one of the causes of the development of the listed medical conditions.

The conventional therapies followed by clinicians to treat depression include psychotherapy, prescription medications, self-help options and certain brain stimulation procedures. However, the above-listed treatment options may not always be sufficient for an individual to recover completely from depression.

In this chapter, we will discuss each conventional therapy and its limitations.

PSYCHOTHERAPY OR TALK THERAPY

Talk therapy or counselling is often the first line of treatment for depression. It's a treatment modality that has been around for years and has helped resolve most cases of depression with regular sessions. But how does it work?

Let's take an example. If you've had a bad day, maybe got scolded by someone or argued with someone, what is the first thing that you will do? Like everyone, you will be sad and want to tell the person closest to you. Why? Because humans need to vent their emotions. We often feel satisfied by speaking to that one person who understands us or is super close to us, isn't it? That person could be our near and dear ones such as mother, father, sibling, best friend, co-worker, or grandparents. It could be just anyone. However, there's a twist in the story when it comes to mental health disorders.

When we have mental health issues, it becomes difficult to convey how we feel. Our speaking mechanism or venting capacity is highly affected. Various reasons can account for this, such as having low self-esteem, lacking self-confidence, experiencing trust issues, engaging in negative self-talk, and lacking self-belief. These factors significantly affect our communication skills and our actions.

That's where therapy comes in. A therapist is a person with whom you can discuss everything. They look at our situation from a non-judgemental viewpoint and suggest solutions that improve the quality of our lives. Speaking to them can not only lighten your heart but also give you guidance that no one else might be able to offer.

If you have never been to a psychotherapist, it can initially feel uncomfortable. However, with time, you may be able to open up to them.

Remember, it is crucial to take one step at a time. Don't be in a haste. If you are not able to figure things out within a few sessions, it is okay. Don't give up yet. Reports suggest that it takes months and sometimes years to get past the trauma.

Talk therapy helps individuals overcome past pain and trauma that may have haunted them for a while. They assist in developing coping strategies that will work for you. You will be able to explore your moods, triggers of your symptoms, and behaviours in a safe place. Therapists will also help you define your goals and get clarity about who you are and what you want from life.

You will be offered a fresh perspective on a long lingering issue. What's more? They also give you an understanding of your emotions and how to better deal with them. Elevating your self-respect, self-confidence, and self-esteem is also a part of their therapy. You can learn communication skills to convey your emotions in a healthy way. Talking to them can give you a new outlook on life.

Psychotherapy has different approaches to address different mental health disorders and benefit different kinds of people. These include:

1. Cognitive behavioural therapy
2. Dialectical behavioural therapy
3. Interpersonal therapy
4. Psychodynamic therapy
5. Self-help Therapies

ANTIDEPRESSANT MEDICATIONS

Doctors prescribe antidepressant medications to patients who suffer from long-term depression and do not respond to counselling alone. They are also helpful for people with advanced symptoms affecting the patient's physical health.

It's unclear how they work. Still, researchers suggest correcting the chemical imbalance in the brain of essential mood and emotion-regulating substances known as neurotransmitters. The most commonly affected neurotransmitters are noradrenaline and serotonin. Antidepressants work towards increasing the availability of these neurotransmitters. In addition, some medications also alleviate pain experienced by people with chronic medical and mental health issues.

The primary goal of treatment with antidepressants is to relieve symptoms such as insomnia, anxiety, arrhythmias, restlessness, and exhaustion and to prevent suicidal thoughts. They only suppress physical and emotional symptoms and do not address the root cause of depression. As a result, they are more beneficial when combined with other conventional treatments, such as counselling.

Most people find relief after several weeks of starting the medicines. Furthermore, antidepressants do not cause addiction or physical dependence. Some limitations of the use of antidepressants are discussed in detail below.

1. **Lack of homogeneity of depression:** Depression presents differently in different individuals. Therefore, many authors suggest that patients should be divided into various categories to make treatment less challenging and more effective.
2. **Side effects of antidepressants:** Even though antidepressants have shown excellent results in improving symptoms of anxiety and depression, patients have reported significant side effects with prolonged use. Furthermore, people develop resistance towards treatment with medication and tend to discontinue them at their own will. Doing that creates gaps in the treatment and often worsens their condition.

References

1. https://www.psychologytoday.com/intl/blog/social-instincts/202102/why-cbt-beats-medication-in-the-treatment-depression#:~:text=Recent%20research%20findings%20suggest%20that,are%20less%20likely%20to%20relapse.
2. https://www.ukessays.com/essays/psychology/benefits-and-limitations-of-cognitive-behavioral-therapy-treatment-psychology-essay.php
3. https://m1psychology.com/strengths-and-limitations-of-cbt/
4. https://www.karger.com/Article/Fulltext/447034

Challenges in Conventional Therapies

With the rise in cases of depression coming to light day by day, researchers are constantly working towards improving the treatment modalities available to people. Each new case comes with its own challenges since each trigger is different, and so is each mind. Every depressed person comes with a different set of reasons for being depressed and requires a unique approach to its resolution.

Standard treatments for depression typically involve psychotherapy, prescription medication, self-help methods, and specific stimulation techniques. Nonetheless, these approaches may not be sufficient for all individuals. Due to the diverse origins of depression, people may need a more multifaceted approach. Some individuals find comfort in sharing their experiences with a therapist, while others may opt for medication to alleviate their symptoms.

But do you think everyone benefits from the above four listed methods to the extent of resolving their deteriorated mental health? No, they don't. Are you wondering why?

Research indicates that while traditional treatments like medication and self-help techniques can be beneficial for some individuals, they often fall short of addressing the root causes of mental health issues like depression. Unlike physical illnesses, such as COVID-19, where medication can target specific viruses or bacteria, depression is a complex mental health condition that stems from various psychological factors.

Our minds are naturally inclined to dwell on negative thoughts and past traumatic experiences. This rumination can lead to persistent feelings of sadness, hopelessness, and anxiety. Therapy, on the other hand, offers a structured approach to understanding and managing these negative thought patterns. By working with a therapist, individuals can learn valuable tools and techniques to reframe their thoughts, challenge negative beliefs, and develop healthier coping mechanisms. This can ultimately lead to healing from past traumas and building resilience against future challenges.

But, the most common issue in treating depression is diagnosing it. Sometimes, certain associated medical conditions may overpower mental health, making it difficult for a clinician to pinpoint the possibility of depression. Moreover, the symptoms of depression are so subtle that they can quickly go unnoticed. When such cases fail to respond to treatment, it is time to modify how we look at the issue. Let us discuss the challenges that conventional treatment modalities pose in treating modern depression disorders.

Challenges that Psychotherapy Pose

Any person who recognizes the symptoms of depression and wants to get treated always turns to a therapist first. A therapist provides unconditional support, care, compassion, guidance and, most importantly, a judgement-free environment to talk about matters that you cannot discuss with anyone else. Professionals who offer therapeutic services are typically known as therapists. However, depending on their level of education and training, they may also be known as counsellors, psychologists, or psychiatrists. The therapy is also known as "talk therapy".

We can categorize psychotherapy into different types based on an individual's specific needs. These include cognitive behavioural therapy, interpersonal therapy, social skills training, psychodynamic therapy, supportive counselling, behavioural activation, problem-solving therapy and family or marriage counselling. Research suggests that all the listed therapies have shown improvement in treating depression. However, they have certain limitations.

These limitations are:

1. Duration of therapy
2. Therapy is not a quick fix
3. Psychotherapy and insurance coverage
4. Personal comfort in talking to a stranger

5. Lack of a specific strategy
6. Homework lethargy
7. Negative feelings while taking therapies.

Challenges that Prescription Medications Pose

As we already know, depression has multi-factorial source of development. It needs individual assessment, which includes a psychopharmacological approach.

People with depression require a team of specialists to rebalance their emotions and return to a normal level of functioning. Most commonly, prescription medicines and counselling control symptoms and improve prognosis. Moreover, individualized treatment also aims at reducing the risk of relapse.

Challenges that Self-help Strategies Pose

Self-help strategies often help when an individual is highly motivated to improve their situation. However, it will work for you only if you are willing to bring a change in your life, be it before or after therapy sessions.

Self-help strategies involve making active changes in life as suggested by professionals, such as replacing traumatic memories with new ones, affirming oneself that "I am enough", changing toxic traits and habits that were leading to the deterioration of the quality of life and developing a positive self-image.

This method is helpful only as long as you are driven by the idea of self-improvement. As soon as the fire of inspiration burns out, you may lose interest in making a change, and there are high chances of relapse. However, self-help strategies are beneficial when it comes to maintaining mental health. It keeps the individual on their toes and improves their quality of life.

Challenges that Stimulation Procedures Pose

When psychotherapy and medications fail to show any changes in symptoms of depression, deep brain stimulation therapies may help. This therapy employs implants, electricity or magnets to trigger brain activity. However, this field is still under research and needs more evidence of its role in treating depression.

These therapies are novel. Patients have reported certain complications such as brain haemorrhage, stroke, headache, infection, speech issues, and problems with motor control or sensory function. This procedure is invasive and has generated mixed opinions among experts, making it a less popular choice for treating depression.

Conclusion

Conventional therapies have been benefiting most people who report symptoms of depression, but they have their limitations. Please note that while traditional methods for treating depression remain effective, some individuals may benefit from alternative therapies. It only indicates the need for innovative strategies to eliminate the root source of the issue and promote sustainable mental well-being.

References

1. https://www.healthcentral.com/article/benefits-and-limitations-of-psychotherapy-for-anxiety-disorders
2. https://www.karger.com/Article/Fulltext/447034

Alternate Therapies for Depression

Mental health takes a lot of maintenance, even after completing therapy with the counsellor or the prescribed medication course. Thus, one treatment or a combination of therapies is not enough to maintain sound mental health. The reason is because there are a multitude of factors responsible for causing depression. Seeking treatment might seem enough, but it isn't. Additional work is needed to sustain it.

Our mental health is analogous to growing a plant. If you want to grow a plant, you don't just sow seeds in the soil. You keep it under adequate sunlight, water it once and leave it. No. You give it the nutrition it needs in the form of fertiliser and water it on a daily basis. If pests attack it, spray it with pesticides and prune the dead parts. In the same way, once your mind is disturbed, you don't just leave it. Instead, you seek treatment and add other modalities that help maintain the new feelings.

Research published in March 2018 suggests that people with depression will benefit from complementary therapies since they have less side effects than antidepressants.

HERBAL REMEDIES

Herbal remedies involve the use of supplements made from natural substances available in nature such as plants. Various products are available for treating various diseases, of which Ginkgo Biloba and St. John's Wort are the most commonly used.

This therapy has gained popularity recently with the intention of using natural substances for managing health. However, herbal remedies do not always imply safety. Therefore, it is essential to know about the product used and its effectiveness in treating your condition.

Research suggests that herbal remedies can help with mild-to-moderate depression and not severe forms.

ACUPUNCTURE

Acupuncture is an ancient technique in which thin steel needles with the width of human hair are inserted at specific spots to provide relief. It has applications in treating many ailments, such as arthritis, cramps, sports injuries, allergies, etc. However, researchers have tried to use this technique to alleviate depressive symptoms.

Acupuncture works by releasing chemicals into muscles, the spinal cord and the brain. Thereby activating the body's natural healing processes. As a result, physical and emotional well-being occurs.

Moreover, acupuncture regulates hormonal imbalances and elevates happy hormones such as dopamine and serotonin. As already established, an imbalance in these hormones causes mood swings and worsens depressive symptoms. Hence, it may help alleviate such symptoms when acupuncture is opted for.

Despite the logic, there is no evidence of the long-term health benefits of acupuncture in treating depression, and more studies are needed.

REFLEXOLOGY

Reflexology is applying pressure to and stimulating points in our feet that correspond to certain body parts. Reflexology is believed to have great health benefits as it promotes healing and releases stress from the body.

Stroking, massaging and applying pressure to affected points can unblock energy flow and relieve tension, as per ancient Chinese philosophy. They believe that when a person is depressed, their energy flow is blocked. Thus, reflexology may help restore the flow of energy and bring symptomatic improvement.

Our well-being is regulated by how we feel and our general health. For example, when feeling extremely emotional, our autonomic nervous system gets activated. When this happens, our body responds by elevating blood pressure and increasing heart rate, signalling stress.

In addition, there is increased production and release of corticosteroids. This hormone affects our neuropeptides, social skills, and behaviour. Thus, in people with depression, we often see elevated levels of corticosterone.

Reflexology is also known to improve blood circulation and break down the build-up of lactic acid crystals in the feet. In addition, many studies indicate that foot reflexology can reduce pain and psychological stress experienced during depression.

So, make sure to seek your doctor's consent before trying out this therapy.

EXERCISE

Exercising is the most underrated and cheapest form of stress buster. When we exercise, our body releases stress. In addition, it increases the production of mood-elevating hormones, which not only add to our happiness but also increase our confidence.

Studies suggest that people with major depressive disorder can benefit from even a single amount of exercise. For example, they concluded that even 15 minutes of cycling could promote mental well-being in depressed people.

Similarly, if you exercise regularly, your body starts releasing feel-good endorphins, which function like natural cannabis and promote a sense of good health. In addition, it helps divert your mind from relentless worries and negative thoughts. It is typically a "breakup" with your cycle of depression and anxiety.

Getting in shape improves your appearance and changes the way you look at yourself in the mirror. Exercising provides not only physical benefits but also psychological benefits. For example, enhanced self-confidence by meeting your goals, even small ones.

Furthermore, the newly obtained confidence allows you to socialise and interact with more and more people, thereby increasing happiness and mood. Lastly, it helps you cope in a healthy way. Which includes not relying on unhealthy habits such as smoking, drinking, vaping and other forms of substance abuse.

MEDITATION

Meditation is a practice that involves aligning oneself. For example, focusing on our breath for even 10 minutes calms our brain activity and keeps unnecessary thoughts at bay.

Meditation keeps your brain calm and allows you to deal with situations in a healthier way. If you meditate during a panic attack or anxiety, it can alter your response to these triggers. Not only does an external response change, but even a beneficiary's physical response can be achieved.

Meditation promotes clarity of thought and improves our focus. It alleviates physical responses to stress and calms physical sensations that we feel when depressed. This practice modifies certain brain regions that have a specific link to depression.

Basically, with regular meditative practice, you train your brain to react to certain situations. It has long-term implications that protect your memory, learning, social interaction, and emotional health.

It's impossible to list all the benefits of meditation. It's something that needs to be experienced first-hand. People who feel lost and feel that they have no sense of purpose can all benefit from meditation. It helps us find ourselves and improves our intuitive abilities. Higher forms of meditation enhance our understanding of self, surroundings, and the universe.

MASSAGE

Suppose you have ever had a massage before. In that case, you may already know that stimulating our muscles has always been a pleasurable experience. Massage increases blood flow to different organs of the body and releases tension.

When depressed or anxious, our muscles become stiff and rigid. As a result, they cause pain and also limit movement. Massage therapists use this technique to relax and relieve tension in the muscles. Massage therapy not only prevents physical pain but also stimulates our brains.

For people with depression, massage won't cure the disorder; however, it will provide symptomatic relief. For example, it will alleviate stress, back pain, sluggishness, and muscle and joint aches. In addition, it can improve sleep and relieve fatigue.

GUIDED IMAGERY

Guided imagery is a simple relaxation technique that relieves stress and anxiety. It's a guided meditation that helps you visualise what you exactly want. Psychotherapists often use it to calm their patients. Still, it can also be practised by common people using YouTube at any time.

The technique is also known as visualisation or guided meditation. Some important benefits of this technique include stress reduction, slowing breathing, lowering blood pressure, reducing heart rate, relieving pain, and decreasing the intensity of depressive symptoms. In addition, it can also put you to sleep.

You can practice this for up to 10 minutes as long as you can maintain your focus. Even if you sleep while meditating, you will still retain all the benefits of the meditation.

AYURVEDA

As already discussed, depression has severe effects on everyday life. Ayurveda not only cures ailments but also provides some treatment options for the symptoms of depression.

Ayurveda offers natural remedies for dealing with stress, anxiety and depression. In addition, many medications are available that help relieve sleep deprivation and stomach-related issues and improve mood and confidence levels.

The ayurvedic approach to depression is according to Kaphaja Unmada. Other milder forms of depression in Ayurveda include pitta and vata.

Even though Ayurveda can help deal with symptoms of depression, it cannot cure it. If you believe that Ayurveda aligns with your body's requirements, you should choose it.

YOGA

Yoga is the practice of aligning one's mind, body and soul. It not only has physical benefits but also elevates the mind and spirit. When practised regularly, it improves focus, increases flexibility, increases self-confidence, helps increase self-love and has many other benefits.

Yoga practices use all or eight limbs of the body. The practice involves relaxation, breathing regulation, physical postures, and meditation. While there are many schools of yoga, some of the most commonly practised ones include Bikram yoga, Iyengar yoga, Ananda, Anusara, Ashtanga, Integral, Kundalini, Kripalu, Power, Sivananda, Vinyasa and Prana. The different types of yoga include spiritual-oriented yoga, fitness yoga, flow yoga, gentle yoga, hot yoga, speciality yoga, and alignment-oriented yoga.

Some of the most important benefits of yoga, especially for people with depression, include increased flexibility, loosening of tight muscles resulting in reduced body aches and pain, improved blood circulation, balancing energies of the body, slowed breathing and reduced heart rate, control blood pressure and cortisol levels, and lowers stress and anxiety levels. Thus, it effectively improves symptoms of many medical conditions such as arthritis, cancer, etc.

A systematic review published by Mehta and Sharma on yoga and depression concluded that yoga benefits as a complementary therapy for depression and its symptoms.

Its applications in treating anxiety and depression still need concrete evidence. However, one can always use it as an alternative therapy to manage symptoms of depression.

References

1. https://www.medicalnewstoday.com/articles/alternative-therapies-for-mental-health-problems
2. https://www.mind.org.uk/information-support/drugs-and-treatments/antidepressants/alternatives-to-antidepressants/
3. https://time.com/3422633/9-natural-depression-treatments-effective/
4. https://my.clevelandclinic.org/health/treatments/9303-depression-alternative-therapies
5. https://www.ncbi.nlm.nih.gov/pmc/articles/PMC5871291/

How do Alternativc Therapies Work? Benefits & Risks of Alternative Therapies

If you search Google for treatment options for depression, you'll find a wide variety of modalities. Why? It is because depression is a complex mental health disorder that needs an individualized approach to treatment.

No two cases of depression are similar since each mind is different, and each person's thought process and feelings are different. The correct treatment methods depend on several factors, such as:

- Current mental status
- Severity and duration of symptoms
- Presence of other physical or mental ailments
- Current medical history
- Ongoing medications
- Patient preference

Conventional treatments such as psychotherapy and medications are the most convenient and effective means of treating depression. However, they have their limitations. Any mental health disorder requires ongoing maintenance beyond medications and therapies. Otherwise, it increases the risk of relapse.

Doctors, since time immemorial, have been implementing complementary therapies such as herbal remedies, meditation, yoga, animal therapy, nutritional monitoring, ensuring adequate exercise, and others to treat mental health disorders. These activities have produced excellent results by elevating the production of happy hormones in the body, boosting mood and lowering anxiety.

These therapies include anything from diet and physical activity to making lifestyle modifications. They promote mental peace and improve the quality of thoughts and life. In addition, they help patients manage symptoms effectively, even when used in combination with conventional treatments. However, make sure to consult with your doctor before implementing any of these.

Furthermore, alternative therapies seem ideal for people who wish to recover naturally instead of taking medications. For milder forms of depression, natural treatments and home remedies help to a great extent. For moderate to severe cases, It is important to note that they should not be relied upon as the sole treatment method but rather used as a supplementary treatment alongside other primary methods.

ALTERNATIVE MEDICINE

Alternative medicine focuses on balancing the mind, body, and spirit to promote overall health. These therapies, often involving energy work, can be beneficial for various conditions, including depression. However, it's important to weigh the potential benefits and risks of any alternative therapy before starting treatment.

Here are some of the benefits of alternative medicine:

- Alternative medicine practitioners emphasise whole-body care and thus provide personal attention to the needs of every individual. In addition, their affordability, philosophies, and one-on-one attention make it more worthwhile for those seeking relief. On the other hand, Physicians struggle to find time for individual attention due to pressure from insurance companies, packed waiting rooms, and limited working hours.
- This modality focuses more on prevention than curing depression, leading to less chances of relapse. While traditional medicine intervenes only once the disease occurs, alternative medicine encourages well-visits, thereby preventing diseases before they occur and caring for you while you are ill.
- Once you have mastered the art, you can independently practice these therapies without any time constraints.

While the benefits sound surreal, it is difficult to accept some harsh truths about alternative medicine. Keep in mind that opting for alternative medicine comes with risks and side effects. However, don't let this discourage you from considering it as a treatment option. It's crucial to stay informed so you can make the best decision for your health.

Keep these factors in mind before you try anything new to fix your symptoms.

- Although the demand for alternative medicine is increasing day by day, sadly, there is not enough scientific evidence about its authenticity and effectiveness in treating depression. Thus, there are many studies underway. Very little evidence is available based on the experiences of the participants of the studies, which has left many questions unanswered.

- You must consult your doctor before enrolling on any of the alternative medicine therapies because they may interact with your ongoing medications or may worsen your associated medical condition.
- Many alternative medicine brands have begun to prioritize sales over the well-being of their customers. They often use catchy buzzwords like "natural" and "safe" to market their products without proper scrutiny. Just because nature is the source of a product, it does not mean that the product is safe for consumption. This is particularly relevant for dietary supplements and herbal remedies, often marketed as "natural" despite their potential for harm. To ensure the safety and efficacy of such practices, there is a pressing need for stricter laws and guidelines to regulate the industry.
- Even if manufacturers of herbal supplements claim that they contain no artificial substances, herbs can still interact with antidepressants and other allopathic drugs. Some supplements may also have side effects of their own.

That is why we recommend discussing with a doctor before investing in such therapies and having full-fledged knowledge about how they will benefit you.

References

1. https://my.clevelandclinic.org/health/treatments/9303-depression-alternative-therapies
2. https://www.helpguide.org/articles/depression/depression-treatment.htm#:~:text=Three%20of%20the%20more%20common,interpersonal%20therapy%2C%20and%20psychodynamic%20therapy.
3. https://www.ncbi.nlm.nih.gov/pmc/articles/PMC3114664/

Role of Nutrition in Mental Health & Brain Function

WHO estimates that by 2030, depression might be one of the top health concerns among the population worldwide. Thus, researchers keep finding new ways to prevent and manage mental health conditions.

We already know that food plays a vital role in nourishing our bodies. To maintain a healthy body, we need to consume essential nutrients like vitamins, minerals, proteins, fats, and carbohydrates. The body cannot produce these vital nutrients, so we must obtain them from external sources.

Have you ever noticed feeling low on energy or mood when you do fasting or skip a meal? Or have you ever seen a hungry friend who snaps at everyone for no apparent reason? These reactions happen because the brain lacks nutrients that are necessary to produce happy hormones in the absence of food. Researchers are thus working specifically on the role of nutrition in brain functioning and the development and treatment of mental health conditions.

Nutritional psychiatry is an upcoming branch of psychiatry that deals with the study of specific nutrients that may trigger depression and help treat it. The two primary questions they are facing are: "Does a healthy diet prevent mental health disorders? If yes, to what extent?" and "Will changing the diet pattern treat these conditions?".

HOW DOES YOUR FOOD TECHNICALLY AFFECT YOUR MOOD?

Serotonin, a neurotransmitter, regulates brain processes related to moods, sleep, appetite, and those that inhibit pain. It's interesting to know that the gastrointestinal tract, commonly known as the intestine, produces most neurotransmitters. The reason is because the stomach is lined by millions of nerve cells. Hence, your stomach and intestines not only digest food but also regulate your mood.

The function of these nerve cells or neurons is dependent on the good bacteria in the intestine. Studies compared traditional diets, such as the Mediterranean diet, to Western diets and revealed that Western diets increased the risk of depression by 25-35%. The reason is that traditional diets consist of vegetables, fruits, whole grains, and other nutritionally high foods as opposed to Western diets that contain sugars, fats, and carbs as primary food constituents.

In addition, these good bacteria in the gut not only influence digestion and absorption but also regulate inflammation, which is directly related to our mood and energy levels.

THE LINK BETWEEN NUTRITION, BRAIN FUNCTION AND MENTAL HEALTH

When we eat, do we think about the effects food will have on our brain function? Of course NOT! We only think of how tasty it is, how soon it will enter our mouth and how satisfied we will be after eating it. Once done, we might also think, "OMG! I've overeaten! My weight will increase!". Isn't it?

Depriving yourself of nutrition is definitely a crime! But food affects not only our weight but also our mood and brain function. It is responsible for regulating the most important functions of the brain. Why torture the wittiest part of you?

It is not only eating habits that affect mental health; the opposite can be true, too. Most of the depressed ones turn to food for comfort. It is easy to hog on less healthy foods such as sweets and processed foods when angry, disappointed or upset. People on antidepressants and anti-anxiety pills also feel the need to eat more since the medications increase appetite and food cravings.

In both these cases, food can come to the rescue. Adding nutrient-rich foods to the diet can alleviate anxiety and elevate mood. However, note that there is no single magic food that will do the trick. A variety of nutrients is a must for optimal brain health.

Several studies in the past indicated an association between the overall quality of the diet and the risk of depression. A review of 21 studies from 10 countries concluded that consuming healthy foods, including fruits, vegetables, pulses, whole grains, dairy, fish and animal food, lowered the risk of depression.

On the other hand, a Western diet of junk food, which includes sweets, refined foods, potatoes, processed meats, red meat, and others, all lead to an increased risk of depression.

Though not significantly proven, indeed, there is an association between mental health and brain function with food.

LOVE FOR PROCESSED FOODS AND ITS EFFECT ON BRAIN FUNCTION

Let's admit it. We ALL LOVE JUNK FOOD. Like, what's not to love, right? Since childhood, we have learned the bitter truth that what we eat to please our taste buds may not always benefit our bodies. Hence, the consumption of processed foods such as fried potatoes, cereals, cheese, tinned fruits and vegetables and other such products are just meant for sale and do not actually do anything good for your body.

Eating naturally available foods, in their raw form or cooked mindfully, helps retain their nutritional value and does the job of maintaining optimal health. Processed foods are high in sugar and flour that train the brain to crave more, as opposed to fruits and vegetables.

Most processed foods are highly addictive. They stimulate dopamine, a hormone and neurotransmitter responsible for the excitation of our brain's pleasure and reward centres. To stop craving such foods, you have to stop eating them. It would be better if you built self-control to bring an actual change in the physiology of the brain.

Functioning of the brain and nervous system totally depends on the nutrition we get from food to build new proteins, cells, and tissues in the body. Hence, experts recommend that you maintain a balanced diet by consuming a variety of fats, proteins, carbohydrates, and minerals. However, you must not stop eating fats and carbohydrates altogether. NO! That would also cause damage to your body. Suppose you cannot do it on your own. In that case, there is always time to learn or seek professional nutritional counselling and fix yourself.

WHAT CAN YOU DO TO BALANCE NUTRITION AND MENTAL HEALTH?

The most straightforward trick to balance nutrition and mental health is learning about the right kinds of nutrition that affect your mood and the way you feel. You must pay attention to what you eat and how you feel after eating certain kinds of foods, which means excluding all kinds of junk foods and sodas and seeing how your mood and emotions are. Try eating clean for two weeks straight.

Plan your meal for the week, and stick to it as much as you can. Start writing a food journal that helps you track what you eat and how much, and add at what time you are eating and the portion as well. In addition, as you get comfortable with the diet, you can add another column about how you feel.

Documenting your emotions and habits gives an insight into your patterns.

If you feel you are overeating due to stress or mood swings, stop immediately. Wait for 20 minutes and gauge your hunger. During those 20 minutes, involve yourself in an intense activity such as walking around the house, outside the house, or drawing; you can also involve yourself in a hobby of your choice. After 20 minutes, if you still feel hungry, eat. But reduce the portion to half of what you thought of eating. For example, instead of eating a whole small packet of chips, start with half. So it can help you control your portions and eat as per your hunger.

We mentioned that it takes around 20 minutes for our brain to signal that we are full and should stop eating. So, we should eat slowly and avoid distractions such as screens to practice mindful eating and become more aware of our body's signals.

So, make sure to write down in your journal all the emotions that you experience when you feel stressed. Stopping yourself from eating excess and writing down how you feel can help you discover what is bothering you. In case you tend to undereat, split your eating schedule into small 5-7 meals a day, instead of three large ones.

It may not always be possible for you to manage your condition alone. If you notice such a thing, seek professional counselling. Asking someone for help is not a sign of weakness or failure; it is the first step towards redeeming self-control and power.

FOODS TO INCORPORATE FOR MENTAL HEALTH BENEFITS

There is no single food that can help improve your brain function instantly. To improve mental health and elevate your mood, you can start by understanding the relationship between a certain variety of food and how you feel after eating it. Then make a plan and start adding foods that helped, and remove those that didn't work for you.

You can refer to the list below to understand which food help the brain function more efficiently and provide the best nutrition for good health. These include foods and habits that come under the category of "clean eating". Add these to your list based on your preference. After trying these, you may realise how emotionally and physically your body has changed.

Here are some brain-stimulating food habits for you to try:

- Magnesium, omega-3 fatty acids and probiotics can significantly improve symptoms of anxiety and depression..
- Eating more complex carbohydrates such as starchy vegetables and rice gives energy. Other nutritionally rich carbohydrates are bajra, wheat, jowar, ragi, and millet. Quinoa and sweet potatoes also keep you satisfied for longer than sugars and processed foods.
- Lean proteins help with quick thinking. Some good sources of proteins are meat, fish, eggs, chicken, cottage cheese, nuts, seeds, and soybeans.
- Fish, meat, nuts, and flax seeds also offer an abundance of fatty acids that are necessary for the functioning of brain and nervous system.
- Avoid eating processed snacks such as potato chips, candies, and soft drinks. These tend to lower body energy and impair concentration.
- Healthy fats are present in olive oil, groundnut oil, sunflower oil, rice bran oil, coconut oil, and avocado.
- Healthy snacks include fruits, nuts, baked or boiled sweet potatoes, and hard-boiled eggs that give more energy than any other food when you feel super-hungry.
- Develop a habit of shopping for healthy stuff and stick to it. Avoid buying unhealthy and processed foods to avoid eating them.
- Don't buy food when you are hungry.
- Eat at timely intervals to avoid feeling very hungry and hogging on food.
- Chew your food slowly, sit in silence and notice how you feel while eating. It will prevent you from overeating. Focus on what you are eating, its taste and its texture. Enjoy every meal you eat.

Conclusion

A healthy and nutritionally well-balanced diet dramatically affects how we think and feel. It gives clarity of mind and improves concentration and attention span.

On the other hand, a nutritionally devoid meal such as junk food and an inadequate diet can impair decision-making, cause fatigue, and delay or response time to situations. As a matter of fact, a poor diet only aggravates anxiety, depression, negative thoughts and mood swings.

However, it is essential to note that mental health deteriorates not only because of food but also because of other factors such as biological factors, genetics, family history, socioeconomic status and life experiences.

References

1. https://www.lybrate.com/topic/the-surprising-role-of-nutrition-in-mental-health-be7d/1b36196d567112c66dc0ba7270c0a2c8
2. https://pubmed.ncbi.nlm.nih.gov/28431261/
3. https://www.health.harvard.edu/blog/nutritional-psychiatry-your-brain-on-food-201511168626#:~:text=Eating%20high%2Dquality%20foods%20that,oxygen%2C%20which%20can%20damage%20cells.
4. https://taylorcounselinggroup.com/blog/the-role-of-nutrition-on-mental-health/
5. https://www.mentalhealth.gov/basics/what-is-mental-health
6. https://www.ncbi.nlm.nih.gov/pmc/articles/PMC2738337/
7. https://thewholeu.uw.edu/2020/03/02/nnm-2020-nutrition-and-the-brain/
8. https://www.sutterhealth.org/health/nutrition/eating-well-for-mental-health

9. https://www.medicalnewstoday.com/articles/nutrition-and-mental-health-is-there-a-link

Who will Benefit from this Book?

IF YOU FEEL A MENTAL FOG?

Lately, if you have been feeling confused, have become forgetful of the smallest of things, and think that you lack mental clarity and focus, you may have a mental fog. When things seem unclear, and you become emotionally demanding, you may need a break. However, if that break also doesn't seem to fix things, it is important you figure out what's wrong. One reason could be depression.

Feeling depressed is not expected since, as it progresses, symptoms worsen and deteriorate routine life. Lack of sleep may be due to stress or tension. Loss of appetite can lead to nutrient deficiencies, which may cause mental fog. Contrastingly, emotional eating, such as overconsumption of sugary foods, fats-rich foods, and others, makes you more prone to infections. In addition, any medical issues, such as thyroid conditions, can worsen mood and ongoing symptoms and cause mental fog.

Some other common causes include excessive eating, a sedentary lifestyle, insomnia, chronic stress and even poor nutritional intake.

If you have experienced any of the above, you will benefit from this book. It may allow you to understand what you are going through and assure you that you are not alone.

IF YOU ARE FEELING FATIGUED?

Feeling fatigued after a long day is normal. However, suppose you are experiencing low energy levels, frequent body aches, lack of clarity, and struggling to find motivation for routine tasks. In that case, you may feel mentally worn down. All these signs indicate fatigue and are indeed screaming for help.

Understand that fatigue is not only due to physical exhaustion; mental fatigue is a thing or too!, It is important to know how to differentiate between the two to know when to seek help and salvage your life.

Usual fatigue is a feeling refreshed after taking a break or taking a short trip. Feeling fatigued for a prolonged period, say, two to three weeks at a stretch, without significant physical exertion, also indicates that you need help. However, if none of it matters, and you feel the same - dull, unhappy, cranky, and emotionally unstable, then you may be depressed. This book is for you if you can relate even a bit to this.

IF YOU HAVE MOOD SWINGS?

Are you feeling up, feeling low? Up again, and then low? That's how mood swings are! An emotional roller coaster. However, when this roller coaster starts affecting your routine life and becomes more frequent than usual, you may need help.

Mood swings are sudden or intense changes in an emotional state. They have plenty of reasons to occur. For example, if you have an illness or injury, or going through some developmental phases in life, have allergies, on medications, are menstruating, have hormonal imbalances, or worse, are depressed and anxious. Each mood swing has a specific reason, duration and approach to cure.

It is not surprising that our eating habits can also cause mood swings. In addition, lack of sleep may sometimes leave us mentally disturbed and screw up our whole day! However, it is alarming that when you develop sudden mood changes, act very irrationally, feel suicidal, or have thoughts of self-harm or harming others, you must seek immediate medical help.

This book will teach you exactly how to recognise the onset of mood swings by noting your timing, symptoms and duration, accepting them and how to manage them in the healthiest way.

IF YOU ARE EXPERIENCING UNRELENTING WORRIES?

Do you identify yourself as someone who worries incessantly about minor stuff? Do simple tasks such as going to the grocery store make you anxious? If your answer is yes, you may have an anxiety disorder. Worrying excessively and feeling anxious over trivial matters is a telltale sign of needing help.

Firstly, know that you are not alone. This book is for those who wish to calm anxiety and find solutions to overcome their symptoms. It works as a guide for passing on genuine and well-researched information about anxiety and depression.

Over 30% of the world's population is estimated to suffer relentless worrying and has been diagnosed with crippling anxiety. When unnecessary stress starts to affect your routine life and prevents you from performing simple tasks, you may be at risk of depression and anxiety.

Some related symptoms include a racing heart, thoughts, difficulty breathing, chest pain, tremors, dizziness, etc. You may also have unnoticed triggers that spark an emotional reaction to insignificant situations.

If you feel you're a target of such symptoms and triggers, this book can help you find answers to most questions that you may have. However, you should use this book only as a guide and not as a method of diagnosis and treatment. We have only compiled information from authentic sources to provide the correct information. For proper diagnosis and therapy, you must still consult a professional.

Why this book?

MANY POPULAR DIETS COME OUT EVERY NOW & THEN, WHICH CONTRADICT EACH OTHER.

With everyone wanting to look and feel good, many people have started digging deep into the "best way to lose weight" or "the best way to get everyone's attention"- suited diets and have started spreading their half-learned knowledge like wildfire. What fuels these diets is the viral reels or videos that promote such diets without much evidence of their benefits.

Switching to aggressive "crash diets" or "keto-diets" from everyday food that our ancestors taught us to eat may have promising results in terms of 'weight loss', but not in terms of mental health. These popular diets neither carry any scientific evidence of benefits nor are they advantageous in maintaining optimum health. Even if they do, their digestive mechanisms challenge the body's natural method and ruin the already well-functioning system.

Staying hungry for long periods deprives your brain of the nutrition it needs to function well. Which, in turn, will make you depressed, cranky, sad, angry, and even low on confidence. Then how on earth do you think they will be beneficial?

In fact, these diets do not even have similarities and often contradict each other. For example, some people recommend following a keto diet that states that increasing the amount of fat intake compels the body to utilise existing fat, thereby reducing weight. However, the body cannot function on only fat intake. It needs other nutrients such as proteins, sugars, vitamins and minerals to perform day-to-day functions. This diet often results in the production of excessive gas, leaving you bloated and unsatisfied.

Similarly, a crash diet is one in which you barely eat anything. Maybe a meal or two in a day. Staying hungry for so long is not advisable. Its immediate effects include fatigue, weakness, inactivity, acidity and bloating. How does this help your mental health? Guess what? It doesn't. It only ruins it.

Hence, ensure that you eat a balanced diet filled with nutrients and minerals to help you grow mentally and physically. Know for a fact that many diets will come and go, but the food that our ancestors taught us to eat will help us sustain and stay healthy.

THIS IS NOT A DIET BOOK, NOR WILL IT TELL YOU THAT FOOD IS A SOLUTION FOR ALL DISEASES, PROBLEMS OR DIFFICULTIES.

We have compiled this book to help you understand your symptoms better. Also, we have gathered and audited thoroughly researched information from authentic resources to spread awareness about the different manifestations of mental health conditions, what triggers and affects each of them, and the various available approaches to treat them.

Furthermore, we have a special section for explaining the relationship between food and depression. This section contains information about how the brain functions and what role nutrients play in regulating our emotions, moods, cognition, and behaviour. This book has also listed foods that contain nutrients essential for the brain.

However, this book does not tell you what diet you should follow or that food will resolve all your diseases, problems or difficulties. For that, we recommend you to consult professionals who can diagnose your condition and suggest how you can treat it. By extension, the book also affirms that you are not alone. It can be used as a guide and support to improve the quality of your life. But do not take it as the ultimate quick fix to your issues, for they may be more severe than you might think.

THIS BOOK IS FOR EATERS

For many of us, life begins and ends at food. If depression affects any of us, it definitely has an impact on what we eat and when we eat. Emotional eating and lack of appetite have been the most consistent symptoms of depression, report studies. Rarely do people with depression eat nutritious food. Therefore, it is difficult for nutritionists to reach their brains, do their job and manage their symptoms. Instead, what happens is their emotions worsen.

Excessive consumption of unhealthy food impairs cognition and fuels depression and anxiety. The same is true for people who overeat or are targets of emotional eating. Such people often hog on unhealthy food rich in trans fat, one of the significant reasons for deteriorating health.

This book is for people who love food and have not been able to keep up with their favourite foodstuff owing to depression. In addition, the book helps you understand the value of nutrients in running the physiological processes of the body. Further, it has tips that can help you cook in a way that maximizes nutrient absorption.

THIS BOOK WILL NOT TELL YOU ANY CHALLENGING PROTOCOL TO FOLLOW OR UNYIELDING DIET PLANS.

Recognizing denial is the first step towards identifying depression. We understand how overwhelming it can be to acknowledge your feelings and accept that you need help. So, congratulations if you have figured out that you need to take charge of your life and turn it around for good! You can use this book as a support and point of motivation to move forward in your mental health journey.

The steps listed are simple and easy to follow. We have neither documented any challenging protocols to follow nor have we suggested any strict diet plans to inculcate in your daily life.

We intend to educate you about the relationship between food, brain function and mental health. This book has tons of information about what precisely each essential nutrient does in the brain, how much you should eat it, and its rich sources.

You must not consider it as a holy grail for guiding you into dieting. But it's definitely the Bible to guide you about what you can add to your meals to refine your mental health.

This book will tell you about the different nutrients and phytonutrients that contain vitamins, minerals & plant compounds to prevent or treat depression & anxiety.

Like vehicles need petrol, our body needs nutrients to run. These nutrients and phytonutrients regulate brain function as well as fulfil other needs of the body. They provide us with the energy required to perform routine functions of the body and actions such as eating, drinking, sleeping, moving, our moods, behaviour, etc.

It is thus essential to learn about the potential role of nutrients and phytonutrients in preventing or treating depression and anxiety. While diet alone is not a replacement for medical treatment for mental health conditions, research has suggested that certain nutrients and plant compounds may play a role in supporting mental health.

Some research has suggested that deficiencies in specific vitamins and minerals, such as vitamin D, magnesium, and zinc, may be linked to an increased risk of depression and anxiety. On the other hand, getting adequate amounts of these nutrients through food or supplements may help support mental health.

Remember that phytonutrients are compounds that plants contain, and research has demonstrated that they can help preserve cognitive function and behaviour in humans. They carry other health benefits, too. For example, certain plant compounds, such as omega-3 fatty acids found in fatty fish and curcumin found in turmeric, have been studied for their potential anti-inflammatory and antidepressant effects.

Overall, a balanced diet rich in whole grains, fruits, lean proteins, vegetables, and healthy fats can provide a variety of nutrients and phytonutrients that may support mental health. However, it is important to talk to your healthcare provider before making any major changes in your diet or starting any new supplements; if you are already receiving treatment for a mental health condition, it is important to be extra cautious. This book will guide you through what you can add to your food list based on your preference, which may help you deal with your symptoms better.

THIS BOOK WILL ALSO MAKE YOU UNDERSTAND THE CONNECTIONS BETWEEN THE FOOD YOU EAT AND YOUR BRAIN.

The food we eat plays an essential role in maintaining the health and function of our brains because our brain relies on a steady supply of nutrients to perform its functions effectively. Therefore, a well-balanced and nutrient-dense diet can help improve cognitive function, mood, and overall brain health.

One of the most critical nutrients for the brain to function optimally is glucose. It is the primary energy source for the brain. Remember that the body derives glucose from carbohydrates in the diet. Consuming enough carbohydrates is crucial to maintain cognitive function and mental clarity. A diet lacking carbohydrates can lead to a decline in cognitive function and mental clarity.

Protein is also essential for brain health since it provides the essential amino acids needed to build and repair brain cells. For example, omega-3 fatty acids found in fatty fish, nuts, and seeds are vital for brain health, as they help reduce inflammation and support brain cell function.

Additionally, vitamins and minerals such as B vitamins, vitamin E, magnesium, and zinc play a critical role in brain function. B vitamins are involved in neurotransmitter synthesis and energy metabolism, while vitamins E and magnesium help protect against oxidative stress and inflammation. Zinc is essential for brain cell communication and function.

On the contrary, consuming a diet rich in saturated fatty acids and trans fats, sugar, and even processed foods has been associated with an increased risk of cognitive decline, depression, and other mental health disorders. These food can lead to inflammation and oxidative stress, damaging brain cells and impairing cognitive function.

With this, we understand that our food can significantly impact our brain health and function. Eating fresh fruits and vegetables, whole grains, and health-beneficial foods can support brain function and protect you against cognitive decline and mental health disorders.

THIS BOOK WILL HELP YOU KNOW THE MOST INFLUENTIAL ACT OF SELF-CARE KNOWN TO HUMANKIND

Self-care has become a popular concept in recent years. However, it is not new. It refers to the deliberate actions taken to maintain or improve your physical, emotional, and mental well-being. These actions result in reducing stress and promoting relaxation.

Sound mental health is a state of well-being in which an individual is well aware of his or her potential, can cope conveniently with the everyday stresses of life, work in a productive fashion, and contribute to the welfare of their family and community.

This book discusses various physical care methods, such as sleeping well, eating healthy, and exercising regularly. These habits will positively impact your mental health. In addition, engaging in other such activities that bring joy and relaxation to you may also help you deal with your situation better. For example, reading a book, drawing, painting, playing a musical instrument or taking a warm bath.

Self-care can also include seeking professional help when necessary, such as talking to a therapist or counsellor. It also includes identifying the signs and symptoms of relapse of depression or triggers that affect your mood.

Furthermore, taking action to fix your situation, such as stepping out of your comfort zone, meditating, exercising, and indulging yourself in other such activities to support your mental health.

In total, self-care and mental health are intertwined. And so, this book helps you recognise your self-worth and energises you to step out of your shell, go out there, and make a difference in your life. Furthermore, incorporating the discussed self-care practices in this book into your life can help you promote a positive mental state and lead a healthier, more fulfilling life.

USING FOOD, IN ADDITION TO OTHER TOOLS, TO EQUIP AND EMPOWER YOU TO LOOK FOR RELIEF IN DEPRESSION AND ANXIETY SYMPTOMS CAN PLAY A SIGNIFICANT ROLE IN RECOVERY

Food can play a significant role in managing symptoms of depression and anxiety but don't consider it to be the only tool to use in recovery. Consuming a healthy and balanced diet regulates mood, reduces inflammation, and provides the necessary nutrients for optimal brain function.

Studies have demonstrated that consuming foods rich in omega-3 fatty acids, vitamin D, and B vitamins can actively boost one's mood. For example, fatty fish, such as salmon and tuna, are rich in omega-3s, which effectively improve the symptoms of depression and anxiety. Vitamin D, found in foods such as fortified dairy products and eggs, has also been linked to improved mood and emotions.

In addition to incorporating mood-boosting foods into your diet, it is also essential to avoid or limit foods that can negatively impact mood, such as those high in refined sugar, caffeine, and alcohol. These foods can lead to energy crashes, disrupt sleep, and exacerbate feelings of anxiety and depression.

While food can be a helpful tool in managing symptoms of depression and anxiety, it is not a substitute for professional treatment. Therefore, it is essential to seek out the support of a mental health professional and develop a comprehensive treatment plan that includes therapy, medication (if necessary), and lifestyle changes, such as a healthy diet and regular exercise.

- The era of sensational and confusing nutritional advice.

In recent years, a lot of sensational and confusing nutritional advice exists in the media and online. With so much information available at a click, it can be tricky to pick what to believe or what advice to follow.

Nutrition science is complex and rapidly evolving. Researchers are constantly publishing new studies that can contradict earlier research, which is the primary reason for the field's complexity. Additionally, experts often have conflicting opinions and beliefs, making it challenging to provide clear and consistent advice.

Another factor contributing to the confusion is the influence of the food industry and marketing. For example, many companies promote their products as healthy or "superfoods," even when little scientific evidence supports these claims.

Moreover, not all information is accurate. Some could even have harmful effects on your body. It is thus crucial to ensure the source you read from is authentic and that you learn about the effect of each nutrient on your body to be able to pick the right food source for a specific nutrient better.

To navigate this confusing landscape, we have performed extensive research to bring you handy, genuine and authentic information to help you recover from your symptoms. We looked for information from reputable sources and experts who base their recommendations on sound scientific research.

Additionally, we have explained the properties of individual foods and nutrients that will help you maintain a balanced diet that includes plenty of beneficial brain health nutrients.

FOOD IS MEDICINE (PHYSICIANS, CARDIOLOGISTS, ONCOLOGISTS, AND UROLOGISTS ARE NOW UNDERSTANDING THE ROLE OF NUTRITION).

Yes, there is growing evidence to suggest that nutrition can play a significant role in managing depression, as well as other health conditions. Many physicians, including cardiologists, oncologists, and urologists, are beginning to recognise the importance of nutrition and its potential impact on overall health and well-being.

The phrase "food is medicine" refers to the idea that the foods we eat can affect our overall health and well-being profoundly. It suggests that food not only satisfies hunger but also actively helps prevent and treat diseases.

Research has shown that a healthy and balanced diet can reduce the risk of chronic diseases such as heart disease, diabetes, depression and some forms of cancer. On the contrary, a diet high in processed and unhealthy food can increase the risk of these disorders.

In addition, some foods contain specific nutrients that have medicinal properties. For example, garlic has antibacterial and antiviral properties. Turmeric contains a component called curcumin that has anti-inflammatory and antidepressant effects.

Some studies have found that a diet rich in fruits, vegetables, whole grains, fish, and other seafood can help reduce the risk of depression. These foods contain important nutrients such as omega-3 fatty acids, vitamin B12, and folate, which have links to better mental health outcomes.

While food cannot replace medication or medical treatment, it can be used as a complementary therapy to improve health outcomes. Many healthcare professionals now recognise the importance of nutrition in preventing and managing chronic diseases. They may recommend dietary changes as part of a comprehensive treatment plan.

IF FOOD IS MEDICINE, IT'S ALSO MEDICINE FOR THE BRAIN.

Food is more than just a source of energy for the body. It is also a powerful medicine that can impact our mental health and well-being. In recent years, with more and more studies going on, people have recognised the link between diet and brain health. Studies have shown that what we eat can have a significant impact on our mood, cognitive function, and even our risk of developing certain mental health conditions.

The brain is an incredibly complex and still mysterious organ that requires a range of nutrients to function optimally. These include vitamins, minerals, amino acids, and essential fatty acids. Therefore, eating a nutrient-dense balanced diet can help support brain health and prevent deficiencies that contribute to mental health issues.

One of the most critical ways that food can impact the brain is through its effect on neurotransmitters. These are chemical messengers that transmit signals between neurons in the brain. These neurotransmitters, such as serotonin and dopamine, are responsible for regulating mood and emotion. Nutrients, like omega-3 fatty acids and B vitamin complex, have been shown to support the production and function of neurotransmitters.

In addition, a healthy diet can also help reduce inflammation in the brain. Research suggests that chronic inflammation contributes to the development of mental health conditions, such as depression and anxiety. Therefore, eating a diet rich in anti-inflammatory foods such as fruits, vegetables, whole grains, and omega-3 fatty acids can support brain health.

In conclusion, if food can improve overall health, why ignore its brain-health benefits? Making small changes to our diet can improve our mood, cognitive function, and overall quality of life.

New Researches

NEW RESEARCHES SHOW THE BENEFITS OF SPECIFIC NUTRIENTS ON BRAIN HEALTH

Nutrition plays a crucial role in the optimal functioning of the body. The brain requires essential nutrients to function properly, and our body obtains these nutrients from the food we eat. Also, scientists have discovered that food may directly correlate with our mental health and impact our memory and cognitive function.

Interestingly, our brain has a high metabolic and nutrient demand. It consumes about 20% of our calorie intake, which, on average, is about 400 calories per day. In addition, the brain is composed of about 60% fat, with high cholesterol and polyunsaturated fatty acid (Omega-3) content.

Neurotransmitters such as dopamine, serotonin and norepinephrine are responsible for maintaining appropriate mental health. The synthesis of these neurotransmitters depends on the levels of amino acids and various cofactors, vitamins and minerals such as folate, vitamin B, calcium, magnesium, Omega-3 fatty acids, and others. Disturbance in any of these may affect mental health.

FOOD SOURCES OF BRAIN ESSENTIAL NUTRIENTS

Have you ever realized that the routine delicacies we eat can be rich in nutrients that are beneficial for the brain? It's amazing how certain foods can play a vital role in improving our cognitive abilities and mental health. Fish and seafood top the charts when it comes to the most nutrient-dense foods you can eat. These have omega-3 fatty acids and vitamin B groups in abundance. If you are a vegetarian, consider adding kale, legumes and beans to your diet, which are excellent sources of fibre, vitamin B group and folate.

To fully benefit from a food item, it is necessary to cook it properly. For example, not covering the food with a lid while cooking causes the evaporation of essential vitamins and minerals.

Inflammation might be important in mediating the link between diet and mental health. Multiple lines of research support the pathogenic role of neuroinflammation in mental illness.

Lucas et al. (2014) used several inflammatory biomarkers and data from food frequency questionnaires to derive the diet that causes inflammation. The inflammatory dietary pattern consists of refined grains, soft drinks, sugar-sweetened soft drinks, red meat, and margarine. Moreover, it is low in olive oil, green leafy vegetables, wine, coffee, and yellow vegetables. Participants who consumed a diet that was consistent with the inflammatory dietary pattern carried an increased risk of developing depression after considering multiple confounders.

HOW DOES YOUR FOOD TECHNICALLY AFFECT YOUR MOOD?

Serotonin, a neurotransmitter, regulates brain processes related to moods, sleep, appetite, and those that inhibit pain. Most of these neurotransmitters are produced in the gastrointestinal tract, which means the intestine, by the millions of nerve cells lining it. Hence, your stomach and intestines are responsible not only for the digestion of food but also for regulating your mood. In addition, the function of these nerve cells or neurons is dependent on the good bacteria in the intestine.

Studies compared traditional diets, such as the Mediterranean diet, to Western diets and revealed that Western diets increased the risk of depression by 25-35% because traditional diets consist of vegetables, fruits, whole grains and other such nutritionally-rich foods as opposed to Western diets that contain sugars, fats and carbs as primary constituents.

In addition, these good bacteria in the gut not only influence digestion and absorption but also regulate inflammation, which directly relates to our mood and energy levels.

BRAIN ESSENTIAL NUTRIENTS

Researchers have been working on formulating a list of Brain Essential Nutrients or BEN. They are also developing a scale that assesses what position a specific food item holds in terms of brain health.

The most essential nutrients that are beneficial for brain health are:

- Long-chain omega-3 fatty acids
- Magnesium
- Calcium
- Fibre
- Vitamin B1, B9, B12 groups
- Vitamins D and E

Not only is it important to add these nutrients to our diet, but it is also crucial to ensure what diet pattern we follow. And this means not skipping meals, eating nutritious foods that fill the stomach and brain mindfully.

Most people tend to skip breakfast, which is the most important meal of the day. It sets the brain's engine on fire and improves our problem-solving abilities and attention span. Moreover, it adds to our energy levels and reduces mood swings.

Hence, you must make the time to cook breakfast and eat well before you leave for work. Another crucial factor is appropriate rehydration. Water is vital for all body processes to function. Dehydration can make us lose our minds and significantly affects cognitive function and attention span. So, ensure that you drink adequate water throughout the day. Now, if you ask how much, you must understand that every individual has a specific requirement for hydration, which depends on the climate, body weight, physical activity, and other factors.

Conclusion

There is no single food that can help improve your brain function instantly. To improve mental health and elevate your mood, you can start by understanding the relationship between a certain variety of food and how you feel after eating it. Then make a plan and start adding food that helped, and remove those that didn't work for you.

A diet focused on Brain Essential Nutrients includes a diet rich in plant-based food items such as spinach, mustard greens, bell peppers, kale, and others. However, it also includes meat such as organ meats, game meats, mussels, clams, oysters, octopus, snails, squid, and fish such as salmon and sardines.

Another critical role in brain health deterioration is excessive consumption of sugars, refined carbs and trans fats.

In order to promote mental health and recovery from mental illness, one could encourage patients to eat a diet that is optimal for brain health. Specifically, this diet would include adequate building blocks for monoamine neurotransmitters, be rich in omega-3 fatty acids, be anti-inflammatory, foster BDNF production, and support a healthy microbiome.

It's important to remember that achieving a balanced diet may seem like a lofty goal, but it's definitely within reach. One practical approach is to focus on consuming nutrient-dense whole foods that contain all the essential vitamins and minerals your body needs. The Mediterranean diet is an accessible template, but it is only one example.

References

1. https://www.ncbi.nlm.nih.gov/pmc/articles/PMC2805706/
2. https://www.ncbi.nlm.nih.gov/pmc/articles/PMC6170050/

3. https://fitminds.ca/brain-health-nutrition-brain-essential-nutrients-and-breakfast/
4. https://www.advancedneurotherapy.com/blog/2015/02/06/brain-function-nutrients
5. https://www.mdpi.com/journal/nutrients/special_issues/nutrition_brain_health
6. https://www.medicalnewstoday.com/articles/324044
7. https://www.health.harvard.edu/healthbeat/foods-linked-to-better-brainpower#:~:text=Research%20shows%20that%20the%20best,%2C%20folate%2C%20and%20beta%20carotene.

RESEARCHES SHOW THAT THE MICROBIOME INFLUENCES MOOD, COGNITION AND RISK OF MENTAL ILLNESS.

Recent researches have revealed that the microbiome, the trillions of microorganisms residing in our gut, influences our mood, cognition, and the risk of developing mental illness. The gut and brain axis is a two-way communication system, implying a constant signalling between the gut and the brain and, indirectly, the microbiome and brain.

Studies have shown that the microbiome can affect mood and behaviour by influencing the synthesis of neurotransmitters involved in regulating mood, appetite, and sleep. In fact, the gut produces 95% of serotonin, and disruptions to the microbiome can cause imbalances in neurotransmitter levels. As a result, mental health disorders like depression and anxiety may either develop or worsen if pre-existing.

Researches have also found that the microbiome can influence cognitive function and memory. Studies in mice report that altering the microbiome can improve learning and memory. In contrast, researchers have associated disruptions to the microbiome with cognitive impairment and neurodegeneration. Additionally, the microbiome can influence the permeability of the blood-brain barrier, which separates the brain from the remaining body and protects the brain from harmful substances. Disruptions to the microbiome can increase the permeability of the blood-brain barrier. Consequently, neurological disorders develop.

Studies were conducted on individuals with depression to test the above hypothesis. Compared to healthy individuals, depressed individuals exhibited significantly lower levels of certain gut bacteria. Earlier studies have proposed a potential association between alterations in the microbiome and an elevated risk of developing conditions like autism spectrum disorder and schizophrenia.

So, how can we support a healthy microbiome and, in turn, improve our mood, cognition, and mental health? The best way, we see, is through making diet and lifestyle modifications. Eating a varied diet rich in fibre, fruits, and vegetables promotes the growth of healthy gut bacteria. In contrast, a diet high in sugar, processed foods, and saturated fats can lead to an overgrowth of harmful bacteria and contribute to inflammation in the gut.

Another way to support a healthy microbiome is through probiotics and prebiotics. Probiotics are high in fermented foods like yoghurt, dosa, idli, and others. They promote the growth of beneficial gut bacteria and improve gut health. On the other hand, prebiotics are a type of fibre that are undigestable by humans but serve as food for beneficial gut bacteria. Foods such as garlic, onions, and asparagus are rich in Probiotics.

In addition to diet, there are other lifestyle factors that can influence the microbiome and support mental health. For example, regular exercise promotes the growth of healthy gut bacteria and lowers inflammation in the gut. Getting enough sleep is also essential, as disruptions to sleep can lead to imbalances in the microbiome and contribute to the development of mental health disorders.

All in all, the microbiome plays a crucial role in influencing our mood, cognition, and the risk of developing mental illness. Supporting a healthy microbiome through diet, probiotics, prebiotics, exercise, and sleep can help improve gut health, promote the growth of beneficial gut bacteria, and reduce the risk of developing mental health disorders. As research continues to uncover the complex relationship between the gut and the brain, it is clear that taking care of our microbiome is essential for maintaining optimal mental and physical health.

References

1. https://journals.sagepub.com/doi/10.1177/0706743719874168
2. https://www.nature.com/articles/s41467-022-34502-3
3. https://www.ncbi.nlm.nih.gov/pmc/articles/PMC6469458/
4. https://www.ncbi.nlm.nih.gov/pmc/articles/PMC5641835/
5. https://www.frontiersin.org/articles/10.3389/fpsyt.2020.585769/full
6. Dinan, T. G., & Cryan, J. F. (2017). The microbiome-gut-brain axis in health and disease. Gastroenterology Clinics, 46(1), 77-89.

If You don't Eat Right, You don't Feel Right

It's a famous saying that you are what you eat. This statement is specifically true when it comes to our physical and mental health. Food is the fuel that powers our body and mind; if we don't eat right, we don't feel right.

If you don't eat well, your mental health can suffer in several ways. For example, suppose you don't get enough nutrients. In that case, your brain won't function as well as it could, leading to difficulties with focus, memory, and concentration, making it more difficult for you to complete tasks or make decisions, which can cause you to feel overwhelmed or stressed.

In addition, if you don't eat enough, your body may go into survival mode, which can trigger feelings of anxiety and depression, meaning your body needs the energy to function, and if it doesn't get enough from food, it will start to break down muscle tissue to get what it needs. That can lead to feelings of exhaustion and lethargy, which can make it challenging to feel motivated or engaged in life.

Overall, not eating a well-balanced diet can significantly impact your mental health. If you're struggling with your diet, it's important to seek help from a healthcare provider or a registered dietitian who can help you make changes to support your overall health and well-being.

Know that the food you eat maintains your health and well-being. Our bodies require a balanced diet of essential nutrients, such as carbohydrates, proteins, fats, vitamins, and minerals, to function correctly daily. Each of these nutrients performs a specific role in the body. Therefore, their deficiency can cause physical and mental health problems.

For example, carbohydrates are the primary source of energy for our bodies. If we don't consume enough carbs, we'll feel tired and lethargic, and our performance will suffer. Similarly, protein is essential for the growth and repair of our muscles, tissues, and organs. Its deficiency can result in weakened muscles, slow injury recovery, and a compromised immune system.

Fats, on the other hand, are necessary for the proper functioning of our brain, heart, and other vital organs. They also play a crucial role in maintaining healthy skin, hair, and nails. A deficiency in essential fatty acids can cause skin problems, hair loss, and other health issues.

Vitamins and minerals are also essential for our overall health and well-being. They are crucial in supporting various bodily functions, such as maintaining healthy bones, regulating blood pressure, and aiding digestion. A lack of these nutrients can lead to a range of health problems, such as anaemia, osteoporosis, and digestive issues.

In conclusion, the adage "you are what you eat" holds true. If you don't eat right, you won't feel right. Following a well-balanced and nutritious diet that includes a variety of whole foods can help support your physical and mental health, improve your mood, and boost your energy levels. By making simple, sustainable changes to your diet, you can feel your best and live a healthy, fulfilling life.

Brain: An Expensive Machine to Run (The Brain Requires 20% of Calories of Daily Intake)

As a complex and powerful machine, our brain needs significant energy to function properly. It requires approximately 20% of your daily caloric intake despite only making up 2% of our body weight. This high demand for energy makes the brain among the most metabolically active organs. Thus, it has significant implications for your overall health and well-being.

Why does our brain require so much energy? At its core, your brain is responsible for carrying out all of the complex processes that allow you to think, reason, learn, and remember. These processes require the rapid transmission of electrical and chemical signals throughout your brain, which requires significant energy.

One of the primary ways that our brain uses energy is through a process known as ATP hydrolysis. ATP, or adenosine triphosphate, is a molecule that stores energy in your cells. When your brain needs the energy to carry out a task, it breaks down ATP into its parts, releasing energy in the process.

Another way your brain uses energy is through producing and maintaining neurotransmitters. Neurotransmitters are chemical messengers that allow your brain cells, or neurons, to communicate with one another. The production and release of neurotransmitters require a significant amount of energy, and so does the process of maintaining the structural integrity of your neurons.

Given the high energy demands of your brain, it is not surprising that your diet can have a significant impact on your cognitive function. Research has shown that eating a healthy and balanced diet supports optimal brain function and reduces the risk of cognitive decline.

One key nutrient that is particularly important for brain health is omega-3 fatty acids. These healthy fats are obtainable through fatty fish, nuts and seeds. Omega-3 fatty acids are critical for the production and maintenance of the myelin sheath, a protective layer that surrounds your neurons and allows for efficient communication between them.

Another essential nutrient for brain health is B vitamins, particularly vitamin B12, found in meat, fish, and dairy. It is necessary for the production of neurotransmitters and the maintenance of the myelin sheath.

In addition, regular exercise also supports optimal brain function. It increases the blood flow to the brain, which, in turn, can help increase the delivery of oxygen and nutrients to your brain cells. Exercise also promotes the production of new neurons and increases the connectivity between brain regions, both of which help improve cognitive function.

Finally, getting enough sleep is also critical for optimal brain function. During sleep, the brain consolidates memories, flushes out toxins, and repairs any damage that may have occurred throughout the day. Chronic sleep deprivation, on the other hand, has been linked to a wide range of cognitive impairments, including memory loss, poor decision-making, and difficulty in concentrating.

In conclusion, your brain is an incredibly powerful and complex machine that requires significant energy to function properly. By taking care of your brain, you can help ensure that you can think clearly, learn new things, and remember important information for years to come.

References

1. https://www.livescience.com/burn-calories-brain.html
2. https://www.scientificamerican.com/article/why-does-the-brain-need-s/
3. https://www.brainfacts.org/brain-anatomy-and-function/anatomy/2019/how-much-energy-does-the-brain-use-020119
4. https://www.ncbi.nlm.nih.gov/pmc/articles/PMC124895/

Factors that Support Optiamal Brain Function

The optimal function of the brain depends upon Vitamins, minerals, fats and proteins for molecules required to back its cells, neurotransmitters and insulating white matter.

The brain is the most complex and vital organ in the body. It regulates and controls nearly every function in your body, from breathing and heart rate to thoughts and emotions. To ensure that your brain is functioning at its optimal level, it requires a variety of vitamins, minerals, fats, and proteins.

Vitamins are essential for maintaining healthy brain function. For example, Vitamin B12 is necessary for producing red blood cells and maintaining healthy nerve cells. A deficiency in Vitamin B12 can lead to memory loss, confusion, and depression. Vitamin D, the sunshine vitamin, gets synthesized in your skin when exposed to sunlight, making it an essential nutrient for brain function. Vitamin D is necessary for synthesizing neurotransmitters that regulate sleep, mood, and appetite.

Minerals, especially iron, are also essential for the function of brain. It is necessary for the production of haemoglobin, which carries oxygen to the brain. Without enough oxygen, the brain cannot function properly. Other essential minerals for brain function include magnesium, zinc, and potassium. Magnesium helps regulate neurotransmitter activity, while zinc is necessary for the production of new brain cells. Potassium is essential for maintaining the proper balance of fluids in the brain.

Fats are also necessary for the function of the brain. About 60% of the brain contains fat. The most essential type of fat for brain function is omega-3 fatty acids. They are vital for maintaining healthy brain cell membranes and regulating neurotransmitter activity. A deficiency in omega-3s can lead to depression, anxiety, and memory problems.

Proteins are the building blocks of neurotransmitters. They transmit signals between nerve cells. The amino acids found in proteins are necessary for the production of neurotransmitters like dopamine, serotonin, and norepinephrine. Proteins are also essential for brain function. A protein deficiency can lead to cognitive impairment and memory loss.

In addition to these specific nutrients, it is important to maintain an overall healthy diet to support optimal brain function. Avoiding processed foods, saturated and trans fats, and excessive sugar and salt intake is also essential.

Staying hydrated is equally important, as the brain requires a lot of water to function properly. Dehydration can lead to cognitive impairment, headaches, and fatigue.

Finally, physical exercise helps maintain healthy brain function. It enhances the blood flow to the brain, improving memory and cognitive function. It also helps regulate mood and can reduce stress and anxiety.

In conclusion, your brain is a complex organ that requires a variety of nutrients to function at its optimal level. Vitamins, minerals, fats, and proteins are all essential for maintaining healthy brain function. Eating a balanced diet rich in these nutrients, staying hydrated, and engaging in regular physical exercise can all help support optimal brain function. Remember to take care of your brain, and it will take care of you.

References

1. https://www.nature.com/articles/nrn2421
2. https://pubmed.ncbi.nlm.nih.gov/16832078/
3. https://www.sciencedirect.com/science/article/abs/pii/S1552526015001010
4. https://onlinelibrary.wiley.com/doi/full/10.1111/nmo.12198
5. https://www.ncbi.nlm.nih.gov/books/NBK507809/
6. https://www.mdpi.com/2072-6643/8/1/6

Start your day with essential nutrients like protein, B vitamins, & choline.

You wake up to a brand new day, ready to take on the day's challenges that come your way. So whether you're heading off to work, tackling your to-do list, or hitting the gym, you need to start your day with the right nutrients to fuel your body and mind.

One of the essential nutrients to consume in the morning is protein. It is necessary to build and repair tissues, produce hormones and enzymes, and support a healthy immune system. It also makes you feel full and satisfied, which can prevent overeating and cravings later in the day.

To get the protein you need, consider adding eggs, Greek yoghurt, nuts, or protein shakes to your morning routine. Eggs are an excellent source of high-quality protein, vitamins and minerals like vitamin D, B12, and selenium. Greek yoghurt is another great option, with up to twice the amount of protein as regular yoghurt. Nuts like almonds, cashews, or walnuts also pack a protein punch, as well as healthy fats and fibre. And if you're in a rush, a protein shake can provide a quick and easy source of protein on the go.

In addition to protein, B vitamins are also important for starting your day off right. B vitamins play a crucial role in energy metabolism, helping your body convert food into fuel for your cells. They also support brain function, mood, and cardiovascular health.

To get your B vitamins in the morning, focus on foods like whole grains, leafy greens, and fortified cereals. Whole grains like oatmeal, quinoa, or whole wheat toast are rich in B vitamins like thiamin, riboflavin, and niacin. Leafy greens like spinach or kale are also full of B vitamins and other nutrients like iron and calcium. And if you prefer a quick and easy breakfast, look for cereals fortified with B vitamins, like bran flakes or oatmeal squares.

Yet another vital nutrient to add to your mornings is choline. This essential brain health nutrient supports memory, mood, and cognitive function. It's also essential for liver function and foetal development during pregnancy.

To get your daily dose of choline, consider adding foods like eggs, soy products, or beef liver to your morning routine. Soy products like tofu or edamame are also good sources of choline, protein, and other nutrients. And if you're feeling adventurous, try adding some beef liver to your breakfast for a rich source of choline, iron, and vitamin A.

By starting your day with these essential nutrients, you'll be setting yourself up for success. You'll have the energy and focus you need to tackle whatever comes your way, and you'll be supporting your overall health and well-being. So why not incorporate some of these foods into your morning routine and see how they make you feel?

Remember, starting your day with the proper nutrients is essential for feeling your best and achieving your goals. So don't skip breakfast, and don't settle for sugary cereal or a pastry on the go. Instead, take the time to nourish your body and mind with protein, B vitamins, and choline-rich foods. Your body and brain will thank you for it.

Another way to ensure you're getting the essential nutrients you need is to plan ahead. Preparing meals and snacks in advance can save you time and energy in the morning and ensure you have healthy options.

In addition to eating nutrient rich foods, hydration is equally important. Water regulates most of our physiological functions, such as appetite, improves digestion, and supports healthy skin and organs. Your goal should be to drink one ounce per kg of your body weight. If you dislike drinking so much water, consider squeezing a lemon, lime, or any fruit of your choice to consume a flavoured drink and vitamin C.

Finally, remember that everyone's nutritional needs are different. Depending on your age, sex, weight, activity level, and health status, you may need more or less of certain nutrients than others. If you're unsure about your nutritional needs, consider speaking with a registered dietitian for personalised advice.

Food is not a Cure for Depression & Anxiety, but it Certainly Helps Support Brain Health

You are what you eat. Especially true for brain health. Just like other organs in your body, the brain, too, needs proper nutrients to function at its best. The food you eat plays a critical role in not only your physical health but also your mental health.

Eating a healthy diet can improve your mood, increase your energy levels, and even reduce your risk of developing mental health disorders. On the other hand, a poor diet can lead to inflammation, oxidative stress, and other negative effects on the brain.

So, what should you be eating to support your brain health? Let's discuss some of the best food options for your brain.

Fish, particularly fatty fish like salmon, sardines, and mackerel, are rich in omega-3 fatty acids. These essential fats are critical for brain health and have been linked to improved cognitive function, reduced risk of depression and anxiety, and even a decreased risk of Alzheimer's disease.

Nuts and seeds are other great sources of healthy fats for your brain. Walnuts, in particular, are packed with omega-3s, while pumpkin seeds are high in magnesium, a mineral shown to improve mood and reduce anxiety.

Leafy greens like spinach, kale, and collard greens are full of vitamins and minerals that support brain function. They are particularly rich in folate, a nutrient linked to improved cognitive function and reduced risk of depression.

Berries, such as blueberries, strawberries, and raspberries, are rich in antioxidant-. They protect the brain from oxidative stress. They also improve memory and cognitive function.

Dark chocolate is a tasty way to support your brain health. It contains flavonoids, which improve blood flow to the brain and enhance cognitive function.

Apart from these brain-boosting foods, it's also essential to avoid processed foods, sugar, and excess alcohol, which can all negatively affect the brain. Consuming a diet high in these items has been linked to inflammation, oxidative stress, and a higher risk of mental health disorders.

Incorporating these brain-healthy foods into your diet doesn't have to be complicated. A few simple swaps can make a big difference. For example, try a handful of nuts or a piece of fruit instead of reaching for a bag of chips for a snack. Instead of processed meat on your sandwich, opt for grilled salmon or roasted turkey breast.

In addition to making healthy food choices, it's also important to pay attention to how you eat. Eating mindfully or paying attention to the flavours, smells, and textures of your food can help you enjoy your meals more and prevent overeating.

Another way to support your brain health through food is to consume home cooked food more often. When you prepare your meals, you have control over the ingredients and can ensure you consume a healthy, balanced diet.

If you struggle with making healthy food choices or don't know where to start, consider consulting a registered dietitian. A dietitian can work with you to develop a personalised meal plan that supports your brain health and meets your individual needs and preferences.

In addition to diet, there are other lifestyle factors that can support your brain health. Getting enough sleep, staying physically active, and managing stress are all important for optimal brain function.

In conclusion, food is the medicine for the brain. Eating a diet rich in brain-healthy foods can improve your mood, energy levels, and cognitive function while reducing your risk of developing mental health disorders.

Incorporating simple swaps and cooking at home can make a big difference in your overall health and well-being. Feel free to seek out the support of a registered dietitian or other healthcare professionals to help you make the best choices.

References

1. https://www.healthline.com/nutrition/6-foods-that-reduce-anxiety
2. https://www.webmd.com/depression/guide/diet-recovery
3. https://www.sutterhealth.org/health/nutrition/eating-well-for-mental-health
4. https://www.aetna.com/health-guide/food-affects-mental-health.html
5. https://www.health.harvard.edu/blog/nutritional-strategies-to-ease-anxiety-201604139441

What is Neuroplasticity?

Neuroplasticity refers to the brain's capacity to form new neural connections and adjust to changes in an individual's surroundings over time. This phenomenon is often called "brain plasticity". Additionally, some regions of the brain are known to be 'plastic', which means they can adapt to changes in response to structural or environmental changes.

Neuroplasticity is responsible for the brain's ability to learn and adapt to new skills, store memories and information, and recover after a traumatic brain injury.

TYPES OF NEUROPLASTICITY

Scientists once believed that the creation of new neurons halted shortly after birth. However, we now understand that the brain can reorganize its neural pathways, create new connections, and even generate new neurons throughout life.

There are two primary forms of neuroplasticity:

- Functional plasticity: It involves moving functions from damaged brain areas to other undamaged regions.
- Structural plasticity: This involves altering the brain's physical structure as a result of learning.

How does Neuroplasticity Work?

During the initial few years of a child's life, the brain experiences rapid growth. At birth, every neuron in the cerebral cortex has about 2,500 synapses or tiny gaps between neurons that transmit nerve impulses. By the age of three, this number increases to approximately 15,000 synapses per neuron.

As people gain new experiences, synaptic pruning occurs, which strengthens some connections while eliminating others. As a result, adults have roughly half the number of synapses as infants. In addition, neurons that frequently form stronger connections, while those that are rarely or never used, eventually die off. By creating new connections and removing weaker ones, the brain can adapt to changes in its environment.

CHARACTERISTICS OF NEUROPLASTICITY

Neuroplasticity has several characteristics that define its nature. Age and environment are significant factors in the extent of plasticity that occurs. The brain undergoes considerable change during early life as it grows and organizes itself, and young brains are generally more responsive to experiences than older ones. However, genetics and environmental factors also play a role in shaping the brain's plasticity.

Neuroplasticity is an ongoing process that involves brain cells other than neurons, such as glial and vascular cells. It can occur due to learning, experience, memory formation, or brain damage. In cases of brain damage, healthy areas of the brain may take over the functions that were previously associated with injured areas.

Nevertheless, the brain has limitations in its plasticity. Specific areas of the brain are primarily responsible for certain functions such as movement, language, speech, and cognition. Damage to these areas can result in deficits because other parts of the brain may be unable to fully compensate for the lost functions.

Examples of Neuroplasticity Adaptations

Neuroplasticity can lead to several adaptations in the brain. The four main types of neuroplasticity adaptations are:

1. **Neurogenesis:** Formation of new neurons in the central parts of the brain, such as the hippocampus and olfactory bulb. Although neurogenesis is more common in the young brain, recent research suggests it can also occur in the adult brain until the tenth decade of life.
2. **Synaptogenesis:** The creation of new neural connections that occur when the brain gets exposed to new environments and experiences. Examples include travelling to new places or learning a new musical instrument.
3. **Long-term potentiation:** The strengthening of synapses through recurring activities such as studying or practising, and it is associated with learning and memory.
4. **Long-term depression:** This depression refers to the deterioration of synapses that remain unused and is associated with memory and motor learning. Neuroplasticity research has investigated the impact of long-term depression on memory loss in neurological disorders like Alzheimer's disease, as well as drugs that impede the prefrontal cortex, such as cocaine.

HEALING THE BRAIN WITH NEUROPLASTICITY

Researches show that neuroplasticity can aid in the recovery of the brain following traumatic injuries. In addition, cognitive rehabilitation and neuroplasticity can assist patients in "rewiring" their brains to enhance their emotional and cognitive health.

Studies on stroke patients have shown that neuroplasticity can help restore lost functions in the brain by allowing healthy areas of the brain to take over tasks from damaged regions. After a brain injury, neurons in affected areas die, and neural pathways become inactive.

However, the brain naturally starts forming new synapses and replacing the dead cells in the days and weeks after the injury. Rehabilitation can aid in this healing process and help individuals recover more quickly.

NEUROPLASTICITY AND ADDICTION

Addictive behaviours such as drug use, alcoholism, and gambling can create strong habits in the brain. The brain can strengthen the neural pathways that support these habits, making them difficult to overcome.

Rehabilitation typically involves replacing addictive behaviours with healthier ones. To break the cycle of addiction, individuals must essentially retrain their brains. The brain's neuroplasticity allows for creating new neural pathways that support these more beneficial habits. In contrast, the neural pathways that support addictive behaviour become less active.

NEUROPLASTICITY AND DEPRESSION

Studies on neuroplasticity have revealed that there is a link between depression and neuroplasticity, much like an addiction. Depression can cause damage to the brain by reinforcing unhealthy neural pathways. This kind of change is known as "negative neuroplasticity."

On the other hand, "positive neuroplasticity" refers to the growth, development and strengthening of healthy neural connections, which has the potential to promote healing. Researchers are exploring ways to stimulate positive neuroplasticity while halting negative neuroplasticity to treat various disorders, including depression, anxiety, ADHD, and addiction.

HOW TO INCREASE NEUROPLASTICITY?

You can divide activities that enhance neuroplasticity into two categories: experiencing new things and practising them repeatedly. Regular physical and mental exercises are to improve neuroplasticity. Certain cognitive training exercises can also promote neuroplasticity. However, the effectiveness of many commercial brain-training products still requires further scientific evaluation. Some examples of activities that may stimulate neuroplasticity are:

1. **Non-dominant hand exercises:** For routine tasks such as brushing or using a computer mouse, you can use your non-dominant hand and encourage the formation of new neural connections.
2. **Yoga:** Practising yoga can decrease stress levels in the amygdala, which is the brain's fear centre.
3. **Reading:** Being exposed to new concepts and vocabulary can increase brain connectivity.
4. **Sleep:** Although sleep is not typically an exercise, getting enough sleep aids in learning and memory retention by strengthening connections between neurons.
5. **Fasting:** Intermittent fasting can promote the growth of neurons and adaptive responses in synapses.
6. **Playing a musical instrument:** Learning a new instrument can help form new neural networks and increase connectivity between different brain regions.
7. **Brain-training games:** Some brain-training games can help improve processing speed, although researchers are still studying their effectiveness.

References

1. https://www.emotiv.com/glossary/neuroplasticity/
2. https://www.verywellmind.com/what-is-brain-plasticity-2794886
3. https://www.britannica.com/science/neuroplasticity
4. https://positivepsychology.com/neuroplasticity/
5. https://www.ncbi.nlm.nih.gov/books/NBK557811/
6. https://www.physio-pedia.com/Neuroplasticity

Inflammation and Mental Health

Inflammation is a complicated biological process that triggers the immune system in response to various stimuli, such as infections, injuries, and chronic ailments. Though it is an essential aspect of the body's immune response, prolonged inflammation has an association with diverse health issues, including mental health disorders. This article delves into the correlation between inflammation and mental health, including its causes, symptoms, and possible treatments.

CAUSES OF INFLAMMATION

There are many causes for inflammation, like infections, injuries, and chronic diseases such as arthritis and diabetes. In addition, lifestyle factors such as poor diet, lack of exercise, and chronic stress can also contribute to inflammation. These factors can trigger the immune system to release inflammatory molecules, such as cytokines, which can cause damage to cells and tissues over time.

SYMPTOMS OF INFLAMMATION

The symptoms of inflammation can vary depending on the underlying cause, but common symptoms include redness, swelling, pain, and heat. In addition, chronic inflammation can lead to a variety of health problems, including cardiovascular disease, diabetes, and cancer. It is important to note that chronic inflammation can also affect the brain and contribute to mental health problems.

INFLAMMATION AND MENTAL HEALTH

Researches suggest that people with mental health issues often have higher levels of inflammatory markers, such as cytokines, in their blood than people without mental health disorders. There is growing evidence that inflammation may cause the development of mental health issues like depression, anxiety, and schizophrenia. In addition, studies have found that inducing inflammation in healthy individuals can lead to symptoms of depression and anxiety.

One theory behind the connection between inflammation and mental health is the "sickness behaviour" hypothesis. This hypothesis suggests that inflammation triggers a series of behavioural changes, such as fatigue, lethargy, and social withdrawal, intended to conserve energy and promote healing. While these changes may be beneficial in the short term, chronic inflammation can lead to persistent feelings of anxiety, mood swings, and negative self-perception.

Another hypothesis suggests that inflammation can disturb the equilibrium of brain neurotransmitters, such as serotonin and dopamine, which are critical in regulating mood and behaviour. Research has discovered that inflammation can limit the accessibility of these neurotransmitters in the brain, which might lead to the emergence of mental health disorders.

POTENTIAL TREATMENTS FOR INFLAMMATION-RELATED MENTAL HEALTH PROBLEMS

There are several potential treatments for inflammation-related mental health problems, including medications, lifestyle changes, and alternative therapies.

- **Medications:** One approach is to use medications that target inflammation, such as nonsteroidal anti-inflammatory drugs (NSAIDs) or immune-modulating drugs. While these medications can effectively reduce inflammation, they may also have side effects and thus should be taken only under the guidance of a healthcare provider.
- **Lifestyle Changes:** Lifestyle changes such as adopting a healthy diet, increasing physical activity, and reducing stress can also help reduce inflammation and improve mental health.

- **Alternative Therapies:** Therapies like acupuncture, meditation, and yoga are highly effective in lowering inflammation and improving mental health. These therapies may work by reducing stress and promoting relaxation, which can reduce inflammation and improve mood.

Conclusion

Inflammation is a complex process that plays an important role in the body's defence mechanism. Researches have shown that inflammation may contribute to the development of depression, anxiety, and other mental health problems by disrupting the balance of neurotransmitters in the brain and triggering a series of behavioural changes. Still, chronic inflammation can cause a wide range of health problems, including mental health disorders.

While there is no single solution for inflammation-related mental health problems, there are several potential treatments, including medications, lifestyle changes, and alternative therapies.

In summary, the link between inflammation and mental health is a complex and growing area of research. While the precise mechanisms underlying this connection are not yet fully understood, it is clear that chronic inflammation can have a negative impact on mental health. Adopting a healthy lifestyle, seeking appropriate medical care, and exploring alternative therapies can lower inflammation and improve mental health outcomes.

References

1. https://www.apa.org/monitor/2021/09/career-lab-depression
2. https://www.psychiatrictimes.com/view/introduction-inflammation-connection
3. https://www.ncbi.nlm.nih.gov/pmc/articles/PMC6529779/

4. https://www.ncbi.nlm.nih.gov/pmc/articles/PMC6658985/
5. https://www.nature.com/articles/s41398-019-0570-y
6. https://cgi.edu/news/surprising-impact-inflammation-mental-health/
7. https://www.psychologytoday.com/us/blog/expressive-trauma-integration/201905/inflammation-and-mental-health-symptoms

Communication between Brain and Gut (that Contains Microbiome)

You may not realize it, but there is a constant conversation going on between your brain and your gut. This communication is known as the enteric nervous system or the gut-brain axis. It is essential for maintaining our overall health and well-being.

The intestine is home to trillions of microorganisms, collectively known as the microbiome. These microbes play a vital role in your health, helping you digest food, produce vitamins, and maintain a healthy immune system. In recent decades, researchers have discovered that the microbiome also significantly affects the gut-brain axis.

The gut-brain axis is a complex network of neurons, hormones, and other signalling molecules that connect your gut and brain. The vagus nerve extends from the brainstem all the way to the abdomen. It is the main highway for communication between the two. This nerve carries signals in both directions, allowing your brain to communicate with your gut and your gut to communicate with your brain.

One of the most significant ways your gut communicates with your brain is by producing neurotransmitters. These are chemicals that transmit signals between neurons in your brain. The gut also produces many neurotransmitters similar to the brain, including serotonin, dopamine, and GABA.

Serotonin, in particular, is a key player in the gut-brain axis. This neurotransmitter regulates mood, appetite, and sleep, among other things. Estimations say that up to 95% of the body's serotonin is produced in the intestines, which helps regulate the movement of food through digestive system.

Another way that the microbiome communicates with your brain is through the production of short-chain fatty acids (SCFAs). When the microbiome breaks down the fibre in your diet, it produces these compounds. SCFAs have a wide range of health benefits, including reducing inflammation and improving insulin sensitivity. They also regulate appetite and energy balance, which can impact your mood and overall well-being.

The gut-brain axis also affects the stress response. When stressed, the body releases a hormone called cortisol. This hormone can have a negative impact on your health if it remains elevated for long periods of time. The microbiome plays a role in regulating the stress response, with some studies suggesting that certain strains of bacteria can help to reduce cortisol levels.

In addition, the axis also affects the immune system. Your gut is home to many immune cells, which help defend against pathogens and other harmful substances. The microbiome regulates the immune system, helping prevent inflammation and autoimmune disorders.

So, what can you do to maintain a healthy gut-brain axis? Eating a healthy diet rich in fibre and nutrients can go a long way, supporting the growth of a diverse and healthy microbiome, which is essential for maintaining good health.

You can also take steps to reduce stress in your life, as chronic stress can negatively impact the gut-brain axis, such as practising relaxation techniques like meditation or yoga or simply taking time to do activities you enjoy.

Finally, you can also take steps to support your gut health directly. Taking a probiotic supplement can introduce beneficial bacteria into your gut. You can also eat fermented foods like yoghurt, kefir, and sauerkraut, which are rich in probiotics.

In conclusion, the gut-brain axis is a complex and essential network connecting your gut and brain. Through the production of neurotransmitters, SCFAs, and other signalling molecules, the microbiome plays a crucial role in maintaining your overall health and well-being. By supporting your gut health and reducing stress in your life, you can help ensure that this communication remains strong and healthy.

It's also worth noting that certain medical conditions can disrupt the gut-brain axis and lead to a range of health problems. For example, conditions like irritable bowel syndrome (IBS) and inflammatory bowel disease (IBD) have links to changes in the microbiome and alterations in gut-brain signalling.

Through the production of neurotransmitters, SCFAs, and other signalling molecules, the microbiome plays a critical role in regulating a range of bodily functions, including mood, appetite, and immune function. By supporting your gut health and reducing stress in your life, you can help ensure that this communication remains strong and healthy, promoting overall health and well-being.

References

1. https://www.ncbi.nlm.nih.gov/pmc/articles/PMC4367209/#:~:text=The%20gut%2Dbrain%20axis%20(GBA,microbiota%20in%20influencing%20these%20interactions.
2. https://pubmed.ncbi.nlm.nih.gov/23010679/
3. https://asm.org/Articles/2023/January/Gut-Microbiome-Communication-The-Gut-Organ-Axis

4. https://www.health.harvard.edu/diseases-and-conditions/the-gut-brain-connection
5. https://www.hopkinsmedicine.org/health/wellness-and-prevention/the-brain-gut-connection
6. https://www.healthline.com/nutrition/gut-brain-connection
7. https://my.clevelandclinic.org/health/treatments/16358-gut-brain-connection

What is an Antidepressant Food Scale?

When it comes to managing depression, medication and therapy are commonly recommended approaches. However, there is growing evidence and also interest in the role of diet in improving mental health. One tool that has emerged in this field is the antidepressant food score, a measure of how well a food or diet supports mental health.

An antidepressant food score is a numerical rating that assigns a value to different foods based on their potential to improve symptoms of depression. This score takes into account various nutrients and bioactive compounds found in foods that impact mental health.

The Antidepressant Food Score is determined using 12 out of the 34 essential nutrients in the diet, including Omega-3 fatty acids (EPA and DHA), folate, thiamin, vitamin B6, vitamin B12, vitamin C, vitamin A, iron, zinc, selenium, magnesium, and potassium.

- Omega-3 fatty acids, particularly EPA and DHA, are essential for proper nervous system function. They have anti-inflammatory properties that help prevent and treat mood disorders.
- B vitamins such as vitamin B6, B12, and folate are involved in the production of brain chemicals that affect and alter mood and other brain functions, and low levels of these vitamins may be associated with depression.

- Vitamins C and A are known for their antioxidant properties, which may positively affect neural pathways.
- Iron plays a critical role in proper brain neurochemistry. At the same time, zinc and selenium have high antioxidant activity and protect the body from oxidative stress.
- Magnesium is an "anti-stress" mineral vital for optimal brain function. At the same time, potassium may help maintain optimal brain function by regulating signals.

The relationship between food nutrients and depression, and the benefits may vary depending on the individual's needs, is poorly understood. That is why the concept of an antidepressant food score is relatively new, and research is still ongoing to determine the most effective way to measure and apply this concept. However, more research is still required.

However, early studies have shown promising results, suggesting that a diet high in antidepressant foods may be an effective complementary treatment for depression.

So, how does the antidepressant food score work and help improve mental health? Let's take a closer look.

First, it's essential to understand that the antidepressant food score is not a standalone solution for depression. Instead, it is an additional support in conjunction with other treatments recommended by your healthcare provider, such as medication and therapy.

There are several factors that can influence your antidepressant food score. For example, certain nutrients and compounds have a more significant impact on mental health than others. These include omega-3 fatty acids, B vitamins, magnesium, zinc, and antioxidants such as vitamins C and E.

In addition, the way that food is prepared and consumed can also impact its antidepressant food score. For example, cooking methods that preserve the nutrient content of foods, such as steaming or baking, may lead to a higher antidepressant food score than methods that decrease nutrient content, such as frying.

So, how can you use the antidepressant food score to improve your mental health? One way is to start incorporating more antidepressant foods into your diet. Some examples of foods with a high antidepressant food score include:

1. **Leafy greens:** Leafy greens like kale, spinach, fenugreek leaves, and collard greens are high in magnesium, which improves mood and decreases symptoms of depression.
2. **Berries:** Berries such as blueberries, raspberries, and strawberries are rich in antioxidants. They protect the brain from damage and inflammation.
3. **Fatty fish:** Fatty fish, nuts and seeds, and others are high in omega-3 fatty acids. They, too, have been shown to reduce symptoms of depression and improve brain function.
4. **Nuts and seeds:** Walnuts, almonds, and sunflower seeds are high in magnesium, zinc, and B vitamins, all of which are important for brain health.
5. **Whole grains:** Whole grains like quinoa, brown rice, and whole wheat bread are abundant in B vitamins. They have proved to improve mood and cognitive function.
6. **Fermented foods:** Yoghurt, kefir, and kimchi are high in probiotics, which improve mental health and reduce symptoms of depression.
7. **Dark chocolate:** Dark chocolate is antioxidant-rich. It improves mood and reduces symptoms of depression in some studies.

Incorporating these foods into your diet, as per your preference, can help improve your antidepressant food score and support better mental health. However, it's important to note that everyone's nutritional needs are different, and what works for one person may not work for another.

It's also important to remember that diet is just one aspect of mental health. Other lifestyle factors such as exercise, sleep, and stress management also play a crucial role in maintaining good mental health.

In addition to incorporating antidepressant foods into your diet, there are other steps you can take to improve your overall diet and support better mental health. These include:

1. **Avoiding processed and sugary foods:** Eating foods that are high in processed ingredients and sugar can cause inflammation in the body, which is associated with a higher likelihood of developing mental health conditions such as depression.
2. **Eating a balanced diet:** This includes eating a variety of foods from all food groups. It ensures that you're getting all the nutrients you need to support good mental health.
3. **Limiting alcohol and caffeine:** These can disrupt sleep and lead to mood swings, making it important to consume these substances in moderation.
4. **Staying hydrated:** Dehydration often causes fatigue and mood swings, drinking plenty of water throughout the day is important.
5. **Talking to a healthcare professional:** If you're struggling with depression or other mental health conditions, it is essential to seek help from a healthcare professional who can provide you with personalized recommendations and support.

It is also important to note that the antidepressant food score is still a relatively new concept. However, incorporating antidepressant foods into your diet can still have a positive impact on your overall health and well-being.

In summary, the antidepressant food score is a measure of how well a food or diet supports mental health. By incorporating more antidepressant foods into your diet, such as leafy greens, berries, fatty fish, nuts and seeds, whole grains, fermented foods, and dark chocolate, you can improve your antidepressant food score and support better mental health.

However, it is important to remember that diet is just one aspect of mental health, and other lifestyle factors such as exercise, sleep, and stress management also play a crucial role in maintaining good mental health.

References

1. https://blog.insidetracker.com/antidepressant-food-score-diet-influence-depression-risk-treatment#:~:text=The%20Antidepressant%20Food%20Score%20(AFS)%20was%20created%20to%20identify%20the,based%20on%2012%20key%20nutrients.
2. https://drewramseymd.com/nutrients/the-antidepressant-food-scale/
3. https://drewramseymd.com/depression-anxiety/heres-the-1-food-category-to-fight-depression/
4. https://www.lemalab.eu/blogs/journal/the-antidepressant-food-score-food-to-help-your-mood-according-to-science

Folate

Depression is a complex disorder caused by numerous factors. Neurotransmitters such as dopamine, serotonin, and norepinephrine are known to be deficient in people with depression. These neurotransmitters are responsible for maintaining stable mental health. Disturbance in any of these affects mental health significantly.

The vitamins and minerals regulate the synthesis of these neurotransmitters, a deficiency of which can disrupt the functioning of these happy hormones.

One of the vital nutrients responsible for regulating mental health is folate, a naturally occurring B vitamin.

Folic acid or folate is a popular vitamin among pregnant women for preventing congenital disabilities. But this vitamin is also being researched for its effects on treating depression.

Studies suggest that a link exists between low folic acid levels and depression. However, their relationship is not an easy one to define, which is why depression is a result of a multitude of factors, and only folate supplements will not help improve symptoms.

TO UNDERSTAND HOW FOLATE AFFECTS MENTAL HEALTH, UNDERSTAND THIS:

Folate regulates levels of BH4, a crucial cofactor responsible for the formation of dopamine and serotonin. Its deficiency lowers BH4 levels and, in turn, reduces levels of "happy hormones" in the body. As a result, if you are already depressed, a deficiency of folate adds up to your depressed state and worsens your condition.

Folic acid also plays a role in the production of DNA and RNA, which are the building blocks of genes. Moreover, it is an active component in the smooth functioning of the central nervous system and brain. Lower levels of folate are also associated with the reduced response of the body to antidepressants in comparison to normal or higher folate blood levels.

Many studies in the past have indicated an elevated incidence of folate deficiency in people with depression. Given that depression is accompanied by a decrease in appetite and loss of weight, simultaneous deficiencies of various vitamins and minerals should not be surprising.

References

1. https://www.ncbi.nlm.nih.gov/pmc/articles/PMC1810582/
2. https://www.psychiatrist.com/jcp/depression/folate-depression-efficacy-safety-differences-formulations/
3. https://www.beatalewismd.com/blog/folate-a-secret-weapon-against-depression

Iron

Iron is an important mineral our body requires to perform vital functions and promote growth and development. It is a part of haemoglobin that carries oxygenated blood from the lungs to all parts of the body. It also allows the muscles to store and utilize oxygen as and when needed. It is a part of other body processes whose disruption affects most physiological functions of the body, including the brain processes.

Research suggests that inadequate and excessive iron levels directly affect cognition and behaviour. That is because iron is mainly responsible for maintaining the high metabolic and energy needs of the brain tissues. The body, especially the brain, requires considerable amounts of iron during periods of rapid growth.

Iron is mainly sourced from the blood in the body throughout life and is variably distributed throughout the brain. If iron levels are low, the brain gets fewer amounts of iron, directly affecting brain function.

Our body is not capable of forming its own iron, and thus, it is important to consume it through food. If the body does not have sufficient iron as per the body's need, iron deficiency anaemia sets in. Anaemia is a condition characterized by the lack of healthy red blood cells, which results in a lot of complications and requires immediate care. People with highly deficient iron may require additional iron supplements to compensate for the deficiency since food may not be enough.

Iron deficiency, in fact, impacts motor function, social behaviour, and cognition. On the other hand, iron accumulation in the brain has a link with ageing, neurodegenerative disorders, and psychosocial disorders. Animals subjected to this condition exhibit evident behavioural dysfunctions and neurological disturbances. These effects may be present due to disturbances in other nutrients as well. It is thus essential to maintain a healthy nutrient intake for overall health benefits.

Some reasons for iron deficiency include poor nutritional intake, excessive loss of blood, and poor iron absorption through food. Young children, pregnant women, or those who are menstruating are highly susceptible to iron deficiency. Interestingly, iron deficiency not only affects various body processes but also impacts mental health to a great extent.

References

1. https://medlineplus.gov/iron.html
2. https://www.ncbi.nlm.nih.gov/pmc/articles/PMC9175715/
3. https://www.google.com/amp/s/www.lybrate.com/amp/topic/iron-benefits-sources-and-side-effects

Omega-3

Omega-3 fatty acids are a type of essential fats that are crucial for optimal health. They are known as "essential" because our body does not produce them; one must consume them through diet or supplements. Omega-3 fatty acids are found in high amounts in fatty fish, such as mackerel, salmon, and tuna, as well as in flaxseed, chia seeds and walnuts.

Studies have shown that omega-3 fatty acids have many health benefits, including reducing inflammation, improving heart health, and supporting brain function. There is ongoing research regarding omega-3 fatty acids, studying their potential to improve mood and alleviate symptoms of anxiety and depression.

While many treatment options are available for depression, including therapy and medication, there is growing evidence that omega-3 fatty acids may also be effective in treating this condition.

Several studies have shown that omega-3 fatty acids can reduce symptoms of depression. A 2018 review of 26 clinical trials found that omega-3 fatty acid supplements were more effective than a placebo in treating depression, particularly in people with major depressive disorder. The review concluded that omega-3 fatty acids might be a useful adjunctive treatment for depression, either on their own or along with other treatments.

The recommended daily intake of omega-3 fatty acids varies depending on age and sex. Still, most health organizations recommend consuming at least 250-500mg per day, which is achievable through the consumption of fatty fish, such as salmon or mackerel, or by taking an omega-3 supplement.

References

1. https://supplements.selfdecode.com/blog/alpha-linolenic-acid/
2. https://www.health.harvard.edu/blog/eating-during-covid-19-improve-your-mood-and-lower-stress-2020040719409
3. https://ajcn.nutrition.org/article/S0002-9165(23)02068-3/fulltext
4. https://www.health.harvard.edu/blog/omega-3-fatty-acids-for-mood-disorders-2018080314414
5. https://www.ncbi.nlm.nih.gov/pmc/articles/PMC5481805/

Magnesium

Magnesium is a mineral in the body, not produced by the body and needs outsourcing. It supports the smooth functioning of the brain. It plays a crucial role in many day-to-day physiological and biochemical processes, such as DNA and RNA synthesis and various cell functions. Other bodily functions include nerve and muscle function, blood pressure regulation, and protein synthesis.

Studies have also shown that magnesium plays a crucial role in maintaining mental health, particularly in preventing and treating depression.

Magnesium is present in abundance in fibrous foods. Some dietary sources include legumes, vegetables like broccoli, green leafy vegetables, seeds, whole grains, and nuts like almonds. Other sources are dairy products, chocolates, meat, and coffee. Hard water, rich in minerals, is also a rich source of magnesium.

If you don't have enough magnesium taken through diet, you may experience deficiency symptoms. Magnesium deficiency can lead to a lot of complications, such as convulsions, fatigue, muscle weakness, abnormal eye movements,etc.

To prevent deficiency of magnesium, regular intake of almonds, spinach, and cashew nuts is important. You can ask your doctor to prescribe supplements if you do not meet the dietary magnesium requirement.

References

1. https://my.clevelandclinic.org/health/articles/15650-magnesium-rich-food
2. https://www.medicalnewstoday.com/articles/286839#_noHeaderPrefixedContent
3. https://www.healthline.com/nutrition/magnesium-benefits#TOC_TITLE_HDR_4
4. https://www.verywellmind.com/magnesium-for-depression-does-it-help-5112650
5. https://www.ncbi.nlm.nih.gov/books/NBK507265/
6. https://chandramd.com/magnesium-supplements-anxiety/

Potassium

Potassium is an essential mineral or an electrolyte found naturally in foods. It is referred to as an electrolyte since it carries a small amount of electrical charge, which activates cell and nerve functions.

One of the most significant benefits of potassium is its ability to boost mental health and alleviate symptoms of depression.

It is a crucial electrolyte that helps regulate your body's nerve and muscle function; it includes the nerve and muscle cells in your brain, which play a critical role in your mental health. When there is deficiency of potassium in your body, it can lead to symptoms of depression, anxiety, and other mental health disorders.

Researches have shown that people with low levels of potassium in their diets are more likely to experience symptoms of depression than those with higher levels of potassium intake. One study found that people with low levels of potassium were more likely to experience symptoms of depression and anxiety than those with higher levels of potassium in their diets.

So, how does potassium help alleviate symptoms of depression? One of the main ways is by regulating the production of serotonin in the brain. Potassium helps regulate its synthesis by supporting the function of enzymes that are involved in its formation.

In addition, potassium regulates the function of the hypothalamic-pituitary-adrenal (HPA) axis, which plays a critical role in your body's stress response. Moreover, it also regulates the function of the cardiovascular system. Hypertension is a common risk factor for depression and other mental health disorders, and potassium can help reduce blood pressure levels.

References

1. https://ods.od.nih.gov/factsheets/Potassium-HealthProfessional/
2. https://www.health.harvard.edu/blog/nutritional-psychiatry-your-brain-on-food-201511168626

3. https://www.heart.org/en/health-topics/high-blood-pressure/changes-you-can-make-to-manage-high-blood-pressure/how-potassium-can-help-control-high-blood-pressure
4. https://www.heart.org/en/health-topics/high-blood-pressure/changes-you-can-make-to-manage-high-blood-pressure/how-potassium-can-help-control-high-blood-pressure

Selenium

Selenium is a mineral that has a significant impact on mental health. Researches also support this and has shown that selenium may be an effective way to alleviate symptoms of depression and promote better mental health.

It is an essential mineral that the body requires in small amounts. It involves various important bodily functions, including DNA synthesis, immune system function, and thyroid hormone metabolism. Moreover, it is a powerful antioxidant, meaning it can help protect the body against damage caused by harmful molecules called free radicals.

Depression can occur due to various factors, including genetics, environment, and lifestyle. It can have a significant impact on a person's quality of life and can even lead to physical health problems if left untreated.

Apart from its effects on depression, selenium has other mental health benefits as well. For example, it may help protect against cognitive decline and dementia, both of which affect the quality of life. Selenium also improves immune system function, essential for overall health and well-being.

References

1. https://link.springer.com/article/10.1007/s12020-014-0477-6
2. https://www.thelancet.com/journals/lancet/article/PIIS0140-6736(00)02490-9/fulltext

3. https://ods.od.nih.gov/factsheets/Selenium-HealthProfessional/

Thiamine

In the journey to conquer depression with food, one essential nutrient that often goes under the radar is Thiamine, also known as Vitamin B1. Thiamine is a water-soluble vitamin, and its presence in our diet can significantly affect our mental well-being.

UNDERSTANDING THIAMINE

Thiamine is naturally found in certain foods, added to others, and available as a supplement. Its role in the growth and function of various cells cannot be understated. Interestingly, the liver stores only small amounts of Thiamine, so it's essential to include Thiamine-rich foods in our daily intake.

HISTORICAL PERSPECTIVE

The connection between thiamine deficiency and health is a recent discovery. In the late 19th century, Japanese sailors experienced high rates of illness and death when their diet consisted primarily of polished rice. These health issues nearly vanished when they shifted to a more diverse diet, including whole grains, meat, beans, and vegetables. Dutch scientists also noted that the chickens that fed polished rice suffered from leg paralysis. In contrast, those on a diet of unpolished brown rice remained healthy. These observations revealed the concentration of thiamine in the outer layers of grains, removed often during processing.

RECOMMENDED INTAKE

For adults aged 19 and above, the Recommended Dietary Allowance (RDA) is 1.2 mg daily for men and 1.1 mg daily for women in the same age group. During pregnancy and lactation, these values increase slightly to 1.4 mg daily. Importantly, there is no established Tolerable Upper Intake Level (UL) for Thiamine due to the lack of reports indicating adverse effects from high Thiamine intake.

THIAMINE AND MENTAL HEALTH

Thiamine plays a vital role in various essential cell functions and the breakdown of nutrients for energy. A deficiency in this nutrient can lead to problems in the brain and heart, both of which require a constant supply of energy. It's essential to maintain an adequate Thiamine intake to support mental well-being.

DIETARY SOURCES

Thiamine is naturally present in foods such as meat, fish, and whole grains. Additionally, products like bread, cereals, and baby formula add thiamine. Here are some common sources of thiamine:

- Fortified breakfast cereals
- Pork
- Fish
- Beans and lentils
- Green peas
- Enriched cereals, bread, noodles, and rice
- Sunflower seeds
- Yogurt

SIGNS OF DEFICIENCY AND TOXICITY

Thiamine deficiency is rare in the U.S. because most people meet the RDA through their diets. However, it can occur from a low intake of Thiamine-rich foods, reduced absorption in the gut, or increased losses in urine, such as with alcohol abuse or certain medications.

A more severe deficiency can lead to conditions like beriberi, which causes muscle loss and peripheral neuropathy, ultimately leading to heart issues. Another condition, Wernicke-Korsakoff syndrome, is often associated with alcohol abuse and can result in confusion and muscle coordination problems. Both types of deficiency can also be present in individuals with compromised gastrointestinal conditions or HIV/AIDS.

DID YOU KNOW?

- High-heat cooking and long cooking times can destroy Thiamine.
- Thiamine leaches into water during cooking or soaking and may be lost if discarded.
- Food processing, such as refining grains, can remove Thiamine, which is why it's added back to many processed foods.

While certain foods and beverages contain Thiaminases, enzymes that deactivate Thiamine, it is extremely rare to develop a Thiamine deficiency from consuming these foods.

References

1. https://www.hsph.harvard.edu/nutritionsource/vitamin-b1/#:~:text=Thiamin%20(thiamine)%2C%20or%20vitamin,thiamin%2Drich%20foods%20is%20needed.

Vitamin C

Depression is a severe form of mood and anxiety disorder characterized by persistent feelings of sadness, loss of interest in activities, and a range of physical and psychological symptoms. This condition affects millions of people throughout the world, and it can significantly impact a person's quality of life. While there are various treatments available for depression, including medication and psychotherapy, there has been growing interest in the potential of vitamin C to alleviate depressive symptoms.

Ascorbic acid is another name for vitamin C. It is an essential nutrient needed for a wide range of bodily functions. It is a potent antioxidant that protects cells from free radicals that damage them, and it also synthesizes neurotransmitters like dopamine and norepinephrine, which are essential for regulating mood. There is evidence to suggest that low levels of vitamin C may be associated with an increased risk of depression and that supplementation with vitamin C may have a beneficial effect on mood.

In conclusion, there is growing evidence to suggest that vitamin C may have a beneficial effect on mood and may help treat depression. However, further research is needed to establish its effectiveness and optimal dosage. As with any treatment for depression, a holistic approach that includes medication, psychotherapy, and lifestyle changes is likely to be an advantageous strategy for managing depressive symptoms.

References

1. https://www.mayoclinic.org/healthy-lifestyle/nutrition-and-healthy-eating/expert-answers/benefits-vitamin-c/faq-20058271#:~:text=The%20link%20between%20vitamin%20C,after%20they%20received%20vitamin%20C.
2. https://www.ncbi.nlm.nih.gov/pmc/articles/PMC8750333/
3. https://bmcpsychiatry.biomedcentral.com/articles/10.1186/s12888-020-02730-w
4. https://www.sciencedirect.com/science/article/pii/S0955286320304915

Zinc

Zinc is an essential mineral needed for a wide range of bodily functions, including immune system function, cell growth and division and wound healing. It is also an integral component of many enzymes and plays a role in neurotransmitter function in the brain. Recently, studies have found that there exists a potential role of zinc in the treatment of depression.

Even though many treatment options are available for treating depression, such as therapy and medication, there is growing evidence that zinc may also be effective in treating this condition.

One of the ways that zinc may help alleviate depression is by regulating neurotransmitter function in the brain. These neurotransmitters are chemical messengers that carry out communication among different nerve cells in the brain. Zinc plays a role in synthesizing and releasing several neurotransmitters, including serotonin and dopamine, which antidepressant medications often target.

In addition to its potential as a treatment for depression, zinc may also help improve overall mental health and well-being.

The recommended daily dietary intake of zinc varies depending on age and sex, but most health organizations recommend consuming at least 8-11 mg per day for adults. Obtain zinc through the diet by consuming foods such as oysters, beef, and pumpkin seeds or by taking a zinc supplement.

References

1. https://medlineplus.gov/ency/article/002416.htm
2. https://www.healthline.com/nutrition/zinc
3. https://www.hsph.harvard.edu/nutritionsource/zinc/
4. https://ods.od.nih.gov/factsheets/Zinc-HealthProfessional/
5. https://ods.od.nih.gov/factsheets/Zinc-Consumer/
6. https://pubmed.ncbi.nlm.nih.gov/7082716/
7. https://www.mdriveformen.com/blogs/the-driven/what-are-the-benefits-of-zinc-for-brain-health
8. https://genesandnutrition.biomedcentral.com/articles/10.1007/s12263-013-0379-x

Choline

Choline is a crucial nutrient essential for many aspects of our health, including brain function, liver health, and cell structure. It is a water-soluble compound that belongs to the vitamin B complex family, and it plays a vital role in several physiological processes. Recent studies have shown that choline supplementation can help alleviate depression and improve mental health, making it an essential nutrient for overall wellness.

Choline has a positive effect on mental health by regulating neurotransmitters that are involved in mood regulation, including acetylcholine and dopamine. Acetylcholine is a neurotransmitter that plays a critical role in cognitive processes, such as memory and attention. Conversely, dopamine is a neurotransmitter linked to pleasure and reward sensations.

Studies have shown a link between low levels of choline and an increased risk of depression. In a study, researchers found that participants with the most insufficient choline intake had a 77% increased risk of depression compared to those with the highest intake, which suggests that choline supplementation may be an effective way to reduce the risk of depression and improve mental health.

CHOLINE HAS A POSITIVE EFFECT ON COGNITIVE FUNCTION IN OLDER ADULTS

It is an essential nutrient that has numerous benefits for overall health and wellness. It can improve cognitive function, enhance liver health, and alleviate depression. Incorporating choline-rich foods into your diet or taking a choline supplement may be an effective way to improve your mental health and cognitive function.

References

1. https://ods.od.nih.gov/factsheets/Choline-HealthProfessional/#:~:text=Choline%20is%20an%20essential%20nutrient,phospholipids%20vital%20for%20cell%20membranes.
2. https://my.clevelandclinic.org/health/drugs/22202-choline-supplement
3. https://www.healthline.com/nutrition/what-is-choline#bottom-line
4. https://www.medicalnewstoday.com/articles/327117
5. https://www.webmd.com/vitamins/ai/ingredientmono-436/choline

Mono-saturated Fatty Acids

Mental health is essential for our overall well-being. Mental disorders, such as depression and anxiety, are prevalent worldwide, and they can significantly impair one's daily functioning and quality of life. While various treatment options are available, researches suggest that nutrition plays a critical role in maintaining good mental health. In particular, the consumption of monounsaturated fatty acids (MUFA) has a positive impact on depression and overall mental health.

MUFA is an unsaturated fatty acid found in foods such as olive oil, avocado, nuts, and seeds. Unlike saturated fats, which can be harmful to health, MUFA is considered a healthy fat. In addition to providing energy, MUFA has several health benefits, such as improving heart health, lowering inflammation, and boosting brain function.

MUFA may also improve the flow of blood to the brain, which can improve brain function.

Despite the many benefits of MUFA, it is important to consume it in moderation. While MUFA is considered a healthy fat, it is still high in calories, and consuming too much of it can lead to weight gain.

References

1. https://www.ncbi.nlm.nih.gov/pmc/articles/PMC6669697/
2. https://pubmed.ncbi.nlm.nih.gov/26613542/
3. https://pubmed.ncbi.nlm.nih.gov/11676990/
4. https://pubmed.ncbi.nlm.nih.gov/25023370/
5. https://pubmed.ncbi.nlm.nih.gov/28450027/

A Brief Note on Phytonutrients

WHAT ARE PHYTONUTRIENTS?

Phytonutrients or phytochemicals are natural chemicals present in plants. They protect plants from insects and radiation from the UV rays. They also have significant benefits for humans, especially those who eat plant-based foods.

Even though they benefit us, they are not essential for life like carbohydrates, fats, proteins, vitamins and minerals. However, they are known to have anti-inflammatory and antiseptic properties. In addition, phytonutrients boost immunity and communication between cells. They also repair damaged DNA, eliminate carcinogens and alter the mechanism of oestrogen.

Researches suggest that consuming a phytonutrient-rich diet can prove to be an effective strategy in lowering the risks for cancer, heart diseases and brain-related disorders.

SOURCES AND TYPES OF PHYTONUTRIENTS

Obtained from natural products such as:

- Fruits
- Vegetables
- Spices
- Whole grains
- Tea
- Beans

- Nuts

Phytochemicals are not essential for living organisms to stay alive. However, their consumption is beneficial to health, especially to diseased individuals. Plants contain plenty of phytonutrients. However, only six are most helpful in humans. These include:

- **Resveratrol:** this phytonutrient is one of the most important ones for cognitive health. It has a link with increased cerebral blood flow.
- **Carotenoids:** These are highly beneficial for immunity and health of eyes. Studies suggest that lutein and zeaxanthin, two of the six carotenoids, are found in the eyes and are known to lower the risk of developing macular degeneration of the eyes.
- **Ellagic acid:** This phytonutrient reduces the risk of cancer and also lowers blood cholesterol levels. It has excellent antioxidant and anti-inflammatory properties.
- **Flavonoids: It** helps protect against cancer and heart diseases. These phytonutrients are responsible for managing communications between cells. They trigger the reduction of inflammation, detoxification, and the risk of the spread of tumour.
- **Glucosinolates:** they, too, like flavonoids, help prevent cancer. Richly found in broccoli, soy, and cauliflower, glucosinolates eliminate toxins from the body.
- **Phytoestrogens:** These mimic the oestrogen functions in the body. It is highly beneficial for women in relieving menstrual discomforts such as hot flashes and other menopausal symptoms. Moreover, it lowers the risk of cancer, bone disease and heart-related disorders.

These nutrients carry abundant health benefits owing to their antioxidant properties, and one should consume them regularly to maintain optimal health.

HEALTH AND BRAIN BENEFITS OF PHYTONUTRIENTS

There are many types of phytonutrients, each with unique benefits. Some of the most well-known include flavonoids, carotenoids, and polyphenols. Here are some ways in which phytonutrients can benefit your health:

1. **Helps lower inflammation:** Chronic inflammation is a major contributor to many chronic diseases, including heart disease, cancer, and Alzheimer's.
2. **Boost immune function:** Many phytonutrients have immune-boosting properties, which can help keep you healthy and reduce the risk of infections.
3. **Improve heart health:** Phytonutrients can also help lower the risk of heart ailments by lowering cholesterol levels, reducing inflammation, and improving the blood flow through the heart.
4. **Support brain function:** Some phytonutrients help improve cognitive function and reduce the risk of age-related cognitive decline.
5. **Improve digestive health:** Some phytonutrients also help improve digestive health. They do so by promoting the growth of beneficial bacteria in the gut and reducing the levels of inflammation in the gut.

References:

1. https://www.healthline.com/health/phytonutrients
2. https://www.unlockfood.ca/en/Articles/Vitamins-and-Minerals/Phytonutrients-%E2%80%93-Nature%E2%80%99s-Natural-Defense.aspx
3. https://www.livescience.com/52541-phytonutrients.html
4. https://www.webmd.com/diet/guide/phytonutrients-faq
5. https://www.verywellfit.com/phytonutrients-phytochemicals-2242002

HOW DO PHYTONUTRIENTS HELP WITH COGNITIVE HEALTH?

Phytonutrients, or phytochemicals, are natural compounds present in plants that provide various health benefits. These compounds are responsible for the vibrant colours, flavours, and smells of fruits, vegetables, grains, legumes, herbs, and spices.

They are not essential nutrients like vitamins and minerals, but researches have shown that they have various health-promoting properties, including antioxidant, anti-inflammatory, anti-cancer, and immune-enhancing effects.

Good nutrition already has a link to brain function. Certain nutrients such as vitamins A and C, iron, iodine, zinc, omega-3 fats, and certain amino acids found in protein are particularly important for healthy cognitive development and ongoing brain maintenance. Recently, food scientists have explored how phytonutrients affect brain health and diseases.

Scientists have also found that phytonutrients play a crucial role in maintaining brain health and managing brain diseases and disorders like depression and dementia.

Several families of phytonutrients potentially promote brain health and well-being in human studies. For example, anthocyanins are present in purple-blue fruits and vegetables, caffeine in different coffee types, L-theanine in green and black tea varieties, and flavonoids in tea, wine, onions, apples, and other fruits.

Moreover, Phenolic compounds are present in a variety of foods, including nuts, fruits, vegetables, grains, herbs, coffee, vanilla beans, and spices. They are all linked to improved cognitive function and the potential prevention of brain diseases like Alzheimer's and Parkinson's.

Many other ways in which phytonutrients benefit brain health include:

1. **Antioxidant properties:** Phytonutrients such as flavonoids, carotenoids, and phenolic acids have antioxidant properties that protect brain cells from oxidative stress and inflammation, which are known to contribute to cognitive decline.
2. **Neuroprotective effects:** Some phytonutrients, such as resveratrol and curcumin, have been shown to have neuroprotective effects, which means they can protect the brain from damage.
3. **Improved blood flow to the brain:** Certain phytonutrients, such as flavonoids and anthocyanins, can improve blood flow to the brain, enhancing cognitive function.
4. **Anti-inflammatory effects:** Chronic inflammation has a link with cognitive decline, and some phytonutrients, such as omega-3 fatty acids and polyphenols, have anti-inflammatory effects that may protect the brain.

References

1. https://www.healthline.com/health/phytonutrients
2. https://www.psychologytoday.com/us/blog/cravings/202205/4-important-phytonutrients-brain-health
3. https://pubmed.ncbi.nlm.nih.gov/30551400/https://pubmed.ncbi.nlm.nih.gov/30551400/

Specific Phytonutrients for Brain Health

CARVACROL

If you are struggling with depression, you may be interested to know that some research suggests that carvacrol, a natural compound found in certain herbs and essential oils, may have antidepressant effects.

Studies have shown that carvacrol can increase levels of neurotransmitters in the brain, like serotonin and dopamine, which are known to play a role in regulating mood. It may also have anti-inflammatory and antioxidant properties, which could contribute to its potential antidepressant effects.

The mechanisms behind carvacrol's antidepressant effects are still poorly understood. However, incorporating herbs and essential oils that contain this compound into your daily routine could be worth considering as a complementary therapy to other treatments for depression. However, it's important to talk to your healthcare provider before making any changes to your treatment plan.

Another potential health benefit of carvacrol is its ability to support digestive health. Studies have shown that it can help relieve symptoms of digestive disorders. For example, bloating and abdominal pain may also have anti-ulcer properties.

Additionally, carvacrol may have potential benefits for brain health. Studies have suggested that it could have neuroprotective effects and improve learning and memory in mice.

References

1. https://pubmed.ncbi.nlm.nih.gov/33854358/
2. https://www.mdpi.com/1420-3049/26/22/6899

CURCUMIN

Turmeric is renowned for its antiseptic and anti-inflammatory properties because of its natural chemical compound, curcumin. It is used as a regular spice in Indian households to add a deep yellow colour to the food. In addition, studies suggest that curcumin has abundant brain health benefits, such as delaying ageing, fighting depression, helping with chronic age-related and memory-related disorders, and others. Moreover, it can alleviate symptoms of various other medical conditions or injuries such as arthritis, sepsis, wounds, etc.

Curcumin accounts for only 3% to 5% of turmeric. This quantity may not be enough though the dietary intake to be effective against depression. Hence, it is advisable to take it in supplementary form. The turmeric supplement contains curcumin and other compounds such as demethoxycurcumin and bisdemethoxycurcumin, which are called curcumin. These have abundant anti-inflammatory effects and may help improve cognition.

Many animal model studies have suggested multiple effects of curcumin on brain health, including normalizing the stress response and enhancing neurotransmitter functions, such as serotonin and anti-inflammatory effects.

Absorption of curcumin does not take place in the digestive tract very effectively. Hence, it needs the addition of certain bioavailability enhancers such as piperine. Pepper, a common spice, contains piperine. Piperine is a very effective anti-inflammatory included in some curcumin supplements. In addition, it aids in the absorption of curcumin.

Curcumin has both anti-inflammatory and antioxidant properties, the effects of which on depression require more in-depth studies.

ANTIOXIDANT

Pain and mood swings are often associated with the presence of free radicals in patients with major depression. Antioxidant foods such as green leafy vegetables, omega-3, turmeric, and others play a role in neutralizing free radicals, thus preventing or delaying depressive episodes. However, this requires full-blown research to implement it as a treatment modality.

References

1. https://www.healthline.com/nutrition/top-10-evidence-based-health-benefits-of-turmeric#:~:text=Curcumin%20boosts%20levels%20of%20the,degenerative%20processes%20in%20your%20brain.

2. https://www.ncbi.nlm.nih.gov/pmc/articles/PMC2781139/
3. https://newsroom.ucla.edu/releases/curcumin-improves-memory-and-mood-new-ucla-study-says

FERULIC ACID

Ferulic acid is a type of organic compound that belongs to the class of hydroxycinnamic acids. Ferulic acid is known for its antioxidant properties, and skincare products, food preservation, and dietary supplements often use it. It is commonly present in various plant sources, such as rice bran, wheat, oats, and coffee.

Ferulic acid is a potent antioxidant, which means it can help protect cells from damage caused by harmful molecules called free radicals. In addition, it has anti-inflammatory and anti-cancer properties. It may also help protect against UV damage to the skin.

Some evidence suggests that ferulic acid may have a beneficial effect on depression. Even then, more research is needed to understand this relationship fully. Studies have suggested that ferulic acid may reduce inflammation in the brain, which takes part in the development of depression. Additionally, ferulic acid may increase certain neurotransmitters, such as dopamine and serotonin, which are essential for regulating mood.

While ferulic acid may have the potential to be a natural treatment for depression, it is important to talk to a healthcare provider before taking any supplements or making changes to your treatment plan. Depression is a complex condition that requires individualized care, and supplements should not be a substitute for medical treatment.

References

1. https://www.medicalnewstoday.com/articles/ferulic-acid
2. https://www.healthline.com/health/ferulic-acid

3. https://www.verywellhealth.com/the-benefits-of-ferulic-acid-89607

THEANINE

Theanine is an amino acid. It is primarily present in tea leaves, particularly in green and black tea. It is known for its calming and relaxing properties and has been used for centuries in traditional medicine for its health benefits. However, in recent years, Theanine has gained popularity as a dietary supplement due to its potential to improve mental health and cognitive function.

One of the most well-known benefits of Theanine is its ability to promote relaxation and reduce stress. It does this by increasing alpha brain wave activity, associated with a state of relaxation and wakeful relaxation. In addition, Theanine also lowers levels of cortisol, the stress hormone. This hormone is known to develop feelings of anxiety and stress.

In addition to its stress-reducing properties, Theanine may also help improve mood and cognitive function. It increases dopamine and serotonin levels, two neurotransmitters important for regulating mood and behaviour. Theanine may also enhance cognitive function by improving attention and memory and increasing mental clarity and alertness.

Another potential benefit of Theanine is its ability to support cardiovascular health. Studies have shown that Theanine may help reduce blood pressure and improve blood flow, lowering the risk of heart disease and stroke. In addition, Theanine may also help reduce inflammation in the body, which can contribute to various chronic health conditions.

References

1. https://www.medicalnewstoday.com/articles/324120
2. https://examine.com/supplements/theanine/
3. https://pubmed.ncbi.nlm.nih.gov/18296328/

PROANTHOCYANIDINS

Proanthocyanidins are a type of flavonoid, naturally occurring plant pigments widely distributed in many fruits, vegetables, and other plant-based foods. Proanthocyanidins are also known as condensed tannins, which refers to their chemical structure - they are composed of chains of flavan-3-ol units linked together through carbon-carbon bonds.

Proanthocyanidins are present in high concentrations in foods such as grapes, blueberries, cranberries, cocoa, and red wine, as well as in certain nuts, seeds, and legumes. They are known to have a number of health benefits, including antioxidant, anti-inflammatory, and antimicrobial effects. Some studies have also suggested that proanthocyanidins may have neuroprotective effects and could potentially help improve mood and reduce symptoms of depression.

Proanthocyanidins have potential effects on depression. Proanthocyanidins can cross the blood-brain barrier and accumulate in certain regions of the brain, where they can exert their beneficial effects.

In addition to consuming proanthocyanidin-rich foods, you may also consider taking a proanthocyanidin supplement. These supplements are available in many health food stores and online retailers and are typically made from grape seed extract or pine bark extract.

If you want to take a proanthocyanidin supplement,it is important to speak with your healthcare provider first. They can ensure that the supplement does not interact with any ongoing medications.

While proanthocyanidins may help improve mood and reduce symptoms of depression, they should not be considered a replacement for conventional depression treatments, such as medication and therapy.

QUERCETIN

Quercetin is a flavonoid compound commonly found in various plants, such as onions, kale, apples, and berries. This natural compound has gained attention in recent years due to its potential health benefits, including its ability to alleviate depressive symptoms. Many treatment options have been available due to a lot of research about the disorder for decades. However, some people prefer natural remedies to manage their symptoms.

These symptoms differ from person to person and are dependent on multiple factors. Conventional treatments for depression include medications, psychotherapy, and lifestyle modifications such as exercise and diet. However, some people may experience unwanted side effects from medications or may prefer natural remedies to manage their symptoms.

Quercetin has many health benefits, including lowering inflammation, improving cardiovascular health, and protecting against certain types of cancer. Additionally, several studies have suggested that quercetin may positively affect mental health, specifically depression. For instance, some researches found that consuming quercetin supplements on a regular basis improved mood and reduced symptoms of depression and anxiety in healthy young adults, as well as those affected by major depressive disorder.

References

1. https://journals.physiology.org/doi/full/10.1152/ajpregu.90925.2008#:~:text=Quercetin%20increases%20brain%20and%20muscle,Regulatory%2C%20Integrative%20and%20Comparative%20Physiology
2. https://pubmed.ncbi.nlm.nih.gov/27651256/
3. https://www.ncbi.nlm.nih.gov/pmc/articles/PMC9027262/
4. https://www.healthline.com/nutrition/quercetin

5. https://www.health.com/quercetin-health-benefits-6825553
6. https://ift.onlinelibrary.wiley.com/doi/10.1111/1750-3841.14317

RESVERATROL

You've been feeling down lately, struggling to find joy in the things that used to bring you happiness. Focusing on work is hard, and even simple tasks feel like a chore. But what if there was a natural way to boost your mental health and alleviate depression?

Consider resveratrol. It is a naturally occurring polyphenol in red grapes, blueberries, peanuts, and other plants. It has potential health benefits, including its effects on mental health. In fact, a study found that resveratrol supplementation significantly improved symptoms of depression in people with major depressive disorder.

This phytonutrient has neuroprotective effects, meaning it helps protect the brain from damage and improves cognitive function, probably because of its ability to lower inflammation and oxidative stress, which can damage the brain and contribute to depression and other mental health issues.

But how does resveratrol actually work in the brain? It increases the production of neurotransmitters, like dopamine and serotonin, essential for regulating mood and emotions. It also activates certain genes and proteins that promote brain health and function.

So, how can you incorporate resveratrol into your diet to reap these potential mental health benefits? One easy way is to drink red wine in moderation, as it contains resveratrol from the skins of red grapes. However, excessive alcohol consumption can actually worsen depression and other mental health issues, so moderation is key.

Another option is to eat foods high in resveratrol, such as blueberries and peanuts—adding blueberries to your breakfast or snacks and snacking on peanuts throughout the day. You can also find resveratrol supplements at most health food stores.

References

1. https://www.sciencedirect.com/science/article/abs/pii/S0166432822004703
2. https://clinicaltrials.gov/ct2/show/NCT03384329
3. https://www.news-medical.net/health/Can-Resveratrol-Improve-Symptoms-of-Anxiety-and-Depression.aspx
4. https://www.ncbi.nlm.nih.gov/pmc/articles/PMC6225181/
5. https://cellandbioscience.biomedcentral.com/articles/10.1186/s13578-020-00491-3
6. https://www.spandidos-publications.com/10.3892/etm.2019.7311

EPIGALLOCATECHIN-3-GALLATE (EGCG)

Epigallocatechin-3-gallate (EGCG) is a powerful antioxidant and anti-inflammatory compound in green tea. Recent researches have shown that EGCG may have a positive effect on mental health, specifically by reducing symptoms of depression and anxiety.

If you are someone who struggles with depression, you know firsthand the toll it can take on your mental health and daily life. Depression is a complex condition that can stem from a variety of factors, including genetics, lifestyle, and environmental influences. While there is no one-size-fits-all treatment for depression, many people find relief from a combination of therapy, medication, and lifestyle changes.

EGCG may be a promising addition to your depression-fighting toolkit. Studies have shown that EGCG has a neuroprotective effect on the brain, which can help alleviate symptoms of depression. Additionally, EGCG regulates levels of neurotransmitters.

In addition to its potential benefits for depression, EGCG may also be helpful in managing symptoms of anxiety. Anxiety disorders affect millions of people worldwide. Anxiety can be debilitating, causing symptoms such as racing thoughts, panic attacks, and avoidance behaviours.

References

1. https://pubmed.ncbi.nlm.nih.gov/35939172/
2. https://pubag.nal.usda.gov/catalog/7019423
3. https://www.sciencedirect.com/science/article/pii/S1756464620303303
4. https://www.frontiersin.org/articles/10.3389/fnmol.2022.1109458/full

5. HTTPS://ONLINELIBRARY.WILEY.COM/DOI/FULL/10.1002/BRB3.1633

LIMONOIDS

Limonoids are a group of natural compounds found in citrus fruits like limes, lemons and oranges, as well as in other plants, such as neem and cherries. They have potential health benefits, including their effects on depression and other mental health conditions.

There are several reasons to believe that limonoids may have potential benefits for mental health. For one, they are known to have anti-inflammatory properties, which may be beneficial for depression. Inflammation has a link to depression in several studies, and reducing inflammation may be a helpful strategy for treating depression.

Limonoids may also have antioxidant properties, which protect the brain from oxidative stress that occurs due to an imbalance between the free radicals and antioxidants in the body, which can damage cells and give rise to numerous health problems, including depression. By protecting the brain from oxidative stress, limonoids may be able to prevent or reduce the symptoms of depression.

In addition to their potential antidepressant properties, limonoids may also be beneficial for other aspects of mental health.

References

1. https://pubmed.ncbi.nlm.nih.gov/30633247/
2. https://pubmed.ncbi.nlm.nih.gov/26763205/
3. https://pubmed.ncbi.nlm.nih.gov/23204645/
4. https://pubmed.ncbi.nlm.nih.gov/24330583/
5. https://pubmed.ncbi.nlm.nih.gov/24086891/

BERBERINE

Berberine is a compound found in various plants, including the barberry plant, goldenseal, and Oregon grape. It is a traditional medicine used in traditional Chinese therapies for thousands of years to treat various ailments, including digestive issues, infections, and inflammation.

Recent researches have suggested that berberine may also have a positive effect on mood and could potentially act as a natural antidepressant. In animal studies, this phytonutrient increases serotonin and dopamine levels, two neurotransmitters known to play a key role in regulating mood.

Additionally, berberine has anti-inflammatory properties, which could also contribute to its potential antidepressant effects. Chronic inflammation often leads to the development of depression, and reducing inflammation in the body may help alleviate symptoms of depression.

Some studies suggest that berberine was able to improve depressive symptoms in rats subject to chronic, unpredictable stress. In addition, the researchers found that berberine was able to increase levels of brain-derived neurotrophic factor (BDNF), a protein that plays an important role in neuroplasticity and the growth and survival of neurons. Decreased levels of BDNF have a link to the development of depression and other mood disorders.

References

1. https://www.healthline.com/nutrition/berberine-powerful-supplement
2. https://www.ncbi.nlm.nih.gov/pmc/articles/PMC6307759/
3. https://altmedrev.com/blog/emerging-research-on-berberine-and-depression-treatment-shows-promising-results/
4. https://www.nature.com/articles/s41598-017-01035-5

Concluding Note

FOOD IS MEDICINE, SO FOOD IS ALSO A MEDICINE FOR THE BRAIN.

Food is a fundamental part of our daily lives and is essential in maintaining our health and well-being. It is the source of the necessary nutrients, energy, and building blocks our body needs to function properly. But food is not only essential for our physical health; it also plays a crucial role in our mental health. The food we eat affects our brain chemistry, which can influence our mood, cognitive function, and overall mental well-being.

THE CONNECTION BETWEEN FOOD AND THE BRAIN

The food we eat can directly influence the gut microbiota, which, in turn, can influence the brain. Researches show that a diet rich in fibre, fruits, and vegetables can promote the growth of beneficial gut bacteria, which can improve mental health outcomes. On the contrary, a diet rich in saturated fat and refined sugars can disrupt the gut microbiota and increase the risk of mental health problems.

There are also specific nutrients that are essential for brain health. For example, omega-3 fatty acids are crucial for brain development and function. They are present in fatty fish, such as salmon and mackerel, as well as in nuts and seeds. Studies show that omega-3 fatty acids improve cognitive function. Additionally, it can reduce the risk of depression and other mental health conditions.

B vitamins are also essential for brain health and help produce neurotransmitters. They are present in a range of foods, including whole grains, green and leafy vegetables, and legumes.

Antioxidants are another essential nutrient for brain health. Antioxidants present in fruits and vegetables protect the brain from oxidative stress.

FOOD AND MENTAL HEALTH

The food we eat can directly affect our mental health, and researches have shown that dietary interventions can be effective in treating mental health conditions. For instance, a study published in the journal *Lancet Psychiatry* found that a Mediterranean-style diet was effective in reducing the symptoms of depression.

The study found that participants who followed the Mediterranean-style diet for 12 weeks experienced a significant reduction in the symptoms of depression compared to those who followed a control diet.

Another study found that a modified Mediterranean-style diet was effective in reducing symptoms of anxiety in adults with major depressive disorder. The modified diet included whole grains, fruits, vegetables, lean protein, and healthy fats, excluding processed foods, sugary drinks, and refined grains.

Apart from improving mental health outcomes, dietary interventions can also improve the overall quality of life. For example, researchers found that a diet rich in fruits, raw vegetables, proteins and other healthy foods was associated with better mental health, physical health, and overall quality of life.

FOOD AND COGNITIVE FUNCTION

The food we eat can also directly affect our cognitive function. Research suggests a diet rich in saturated fat and refined sugar can impair cognitive function. The study also found that a diet high in saturated fat and sugar was associated with poorer cognitive function.

Another study published in the *American Journal of Clinical Nutrition* suggests that a diet rich in omega-3 fatty acids improves cognitive function in older adults. The study found that participants who consumed a diet high in omega-3 fatty acids had better cognitive function than those who consumed a diet low in omega-3 fatty acids.

FOOD AND BRAIN DEVELOPMENT

The food we eat during early childhood and adolescence can have a significant impact on brain development. Nutrients like vitamin B complex, omega-3 fatty acids, and antioxidants are essential for brain development and function.

Conclusion

Food is medicine and plays a crucial role in supporting our mental health and cognitive function. The gut-brain axis connects the gut and the brain, and the food we eat can directly influence this connection. A diet rich in fibre, fruits, vegetables, whole grains, lean protein, and healthy fats can promote the growth of beneficial gut bacteria and support mental health outcomes.

Eating a healthy diet is essential for supporting mental health, cognitive function, and overall well-being. Dietary interventions are effective in treating mental health conditions and improving the overall quality of life. Nutrients that are essential for brain health, if taken, can improve cognitive function.

References

1. https://www.ncbi.nlm.nih.gov/pmc/articles/PMC7322667/
2. https://newsroom.ucla.edu/magazine/food-as-brain-medicine-gomez-pinilla
3. https://www.chop.edu/health-resources/food-medicine-supporting-brain-health
4. https://www.health.harvard.edu/blog/nutritional-psychiatry-your-brain-on-food-201511168626
5. https://www.everydayhealth.com/diet-nutrition/food-as-medicine-what-it-means-and-how-to-reap-the-benefits/
6. https://www.healthline.com/nutrition/food-as-medicine

CHOOSING FOOD IS IN YOUR HAND

Food maintains our physical and mental health. Many researches have shown that our diet can significantly affect our mood and mental well-being. In particular, certain foods can help combat depression, too. Let us explore the link between diet and depression, the best foods to eat for mental health, and how to incorporate these foods into your diet.

Depression is a debilitating mental health disorder. Studies have found that eating processed and refined foods, sugar, and saturated fat increases the risk of depression. In contrast, a diet rich in whole wheats, vegetables, fruits, and proteins has a lower risk of depression.

One of the reasons that diet affects mood is due to the gut-brain axis. This axis is a complex communication network between the gut and the brain, involving the immune system, hormones, and neurotransmitters.

Studies indicate that specific foods can aid in maintaining a healthy gut microbiome and enhance one's mood. Omega-3 fatty acids, a crucial nutrient for brain health, are among the most beneficial foods for mental health. Fatty fish, like salmon, tuna, and sardines, along with nuts and seeds such as walnuts, chia seeds, and flaxseeds, are excellent sources of omega-3 fatty acids. These nutrients are known to reduce symptoms of depression and anxiety while also decreasing inflammation in the body, which is a contributing factor to depression.

Vitamin D, a crucial nutrient for mental well-being, is produced by the body when exposed to sunlight. Insufficient levels of vitamin D have a link to a higher likelihood of depression and other mood disorders. Food containing high amounts of vitamin D include fatty fish, egg yolks, and mushrooms. Nevertheless, acquiring enough vitamin D through diet alone can be difficult, particularly in the winter months or in an area with limited sun exposure. In such cases, taking a vitamin D supplement might be necessary.

In addition to omega-3 fatty acids and vitamin D, other nutrients that are important for mental health include B vitamins, magnesium, and zinc. B vitamins produce serotonin and dopamine, while magnesium and zinc are necessary for regulating the nervous system. Foods rich in B vitamins include whole grains, leafy greens, and legumes, while magnesium is present in nuts, seeds, and leafy greens. Zinc is abundant in oysters, red meat, and poultry.

While these nutrients are crucial for mental health, focusing on whole foods and a balanced diet is essential. Eating a variety of foods is also important, as different foods contain different nutrients that are necessary for optimal health.

Avoid processed and unhealthy foods and focus on gut health to improve mood and reduce the risk of depression. In addition to diet, other lifestyle factors such as exercise, sleep, stress reduction, and social support are also essential for mental well-being. You can improve your mood and overall quality of life by making small changes to your lifestyle and food habits.

References

1. https://www.ncbi.nlm.nih.gov/pmc/articles/PMC2738337/
2. http://www.cardiacwellnessinstitute.com/heart-disease-treatment-prevention/tag/depression/
3. https://www.aetna.com/health-guide/food-affects-mental-health.html
4. https://kidshealth.org/en/teens/emotional-eating.html
5. https://www.everydayhealth.com/depression/tips-for-eating-well-when-cooking-feels-impossible/

OPT FOR NUTRIENT-DENSE FOOD.

Are you struggling with depression? If so, one aspect of your mental health that you may not have considered is the role that your diet plays. It's important to note that food is not a cure for depression, and you should always work with a mental health professional to address your mental health concerns. However, incorporating nutrient-dense foods into your diet can support your overall health and potentially improve your symptoms of depression.

So, what are nutrient-dense foods? Nutrient-dense foods are those foods that contain high amounts of nutrients related to their calorie content. Essentially, they provide a lot of bang for your buck in terms of nutrition. Some examples of nutrient-dense foods include whole grains, lean proteins, and healthy fats.

Researches have suggested that a diet high in nutrient-dense foods may be beneficial for those with depression. A study found that individuals who followed a diet high in fruits and vegetables like green leafy veggies, nuts and seeds, eggs, etc., had lower rates of depression when compared to those who consumed a diet high in processed foods, sugary drinks, and fried foods.

Nutrient-dense foods may have a positive effect on depression due to the presence of brain-healthy nutrients. Omega-3 fatty acids in fatty fish like sardines and salmon possess anti-inflammatory properties and could help alleviate depressive symptoms.

Vitamin D is not only necessary for bone health, but it also helps regulate mood. Moreover, studies have indicated that vitamin D toxicity-induced hypercalcemia may also contribute to depression. Foods such as egg yolks, fortified products like milk and cereals, and fatty fish provide a rich source of vitamin D.

There is no single food that can help improve your brain function instantly. To improve mental health and elevate your mood, you can start by understanding the relationship between a certain variety of foods and how you feel after eating them. Then, make a plan, add foods that helped, and remove those that didn't work for you.

You can refer to the list below to understand which foods help the brain function more efficiently and provide the best nutrition for good health. These include foods and habits that come under the category of "clean eating". Add these to your list based on your preference. After trying these, you may realize how emotionally and physically your body has changed.

Here are some brain-stimulating food habits for you to try:

- Magnesium, omega-3 fatty acids and probiotics can improve symptoms of anxiety and depression significantly.

- Avoid eating processed snacks such as potato chips, candies, and soft drinks. These tend to lower body energy and impair concentration.
- Healthy fats are present in olive oil, groundnut oil, sunflower oil, rice bran oil, coconut oil and avocado.
- Healthy snacks include fruits, nuts, baked or boiled sweet potatoes, and hard-boiled eggs that give more energy than any other foods for times when you feel super-hungry.
- Develop a habit of shopping for healthy stuff and stick to it. Avoid buying unhealthy and processed food to avoid eating them.
- Don't buy food when you are hungry.
- Eat at timely intervals to avoid feeling very hungry and hogging on food.
- Chew your food slowly, sit silently, and notice how you feel while eating; it will prevent you from overeating. Focus on what you are eating, its taste and its texture. Enjoy every meal you eat. While food is not a cure for depression, incorporating nutrient-dense foods into your diet can support overall health and potentially improve symptoms of depression.

References

1. https://www.nature.com/articles/nrn2421
2. https://bmcmedicine.biomedcentral.com/articles/10.1186/s12916-017-0791-y
3. https://bmcmedicine.biomedcentral.com/articles/10.1186/s12916-015-0428-y
4. https://www.health.harvard.edu/blog/nutritional-psychiatry-your-brain-on-food-201511168626
5. https://www.mdpi.com/2072-6643/8/12/759

3

Essential Brain-Building Nutrients

The human brain is a complex and unique organ that is responsible for controlling every aspect of our body and mind. Despite being only about 3 pounds in weight, it contains billions of specialized cells known as neurons and glial cells that work together to allow us to think, feel, move, and interact with the world around us.

The neurons in the brain are the basic building blocks of the nervous system. They are specialized cells that transmit electrical and chemical signals to other neurons, muscle cells, and bodily glands. There are several different types of neurons, each with a specific function. For example, sensory neurons carry information from sensory receptors in the body to the brain, motor neurons carry signals from the brain to muscles, and interneurons connect neurons within the brain and spinal cord.

In addition to neurons, the glial cells in the brain play a crucial role in supporting the nervous system. These are of many types, including astrocytes, oligodendrocytes, and microglia. Astrocytes provide structural support to neurons and help regulate the brain's chemical environment. Oligodendrocytes produce myelin, a fatty substance that covers the axons of neurons and helps speed up electrical signal transmission. Microglia are the cells responsible for the brain's immunity. They help protect against infection and inflammation.

The brain has several distinct regions that perform specific functions. The cerebrum's two hemispheres, the brain's largest region, are responsible for conscious thought, perception, sensation, and voluntary movement. The cerebellum, located under the cerebrum, coordinates movement and balance. The brainstem is the organ that connects the brain to the spinal cord. It is responsible for controlling basic life-sustaining functions such as breathing and heart rate.

Within the cerebrum are several different lobes, each with a specific function. The frontal lobe, located at the front of the brain, controls executive functions such as decision-making, planning, and problem-solving.

The parietal lobe, located at the top and back of the brain, is responsible for processing sensory information from the body. The temporal lobe, located on the sides of the brain, processes auditory information and memory. The occipital lobe, located at the back of the brain, processes visual information.

Several different structures within the brain play important roles in various functions. The hippocampus, located in the temporal lobe, forms and stores new memories. The amygdala in the temporal lobe processes emotions, particularly fear and aggression. The hypothalamus is a small but important part of the brain in the brainstem. It regulates various physiological processes, such as hunger, thirst, and body temperature.

Although we have gained knowledge about the brain, there is still a vast amount of information we still need to learn. As a result, researchers are actively studying the brain to enhance our comprehension of its intricate functions and to establish novel treatments for neurological and psychiatric illnesses.

Cognitive Stimulation

Mental exercise, also known as cognitive stimulation, refers to activities that challenge the brain and promote mental fitness. Just as physical exercise is important for maintaining physical health, mental exercise is essential for maintaining cognitive health.

Engaging in mental exercise can help improve various cognitive abilities, such as attention, memory, problem-solving, and decision-making. It can also help delay or prevent cognitive decline and lower the risk of developing neurological disorders.

Mental exercise can take many forms, including reading, playing games, learning a new skill, socializing, and engaging in hobbies or activities that require mental effort. The key is choosing challenging activities that require the brain to work hard.

Researches have shown that mental exercise strengthens the connections between neurons in the brain, increases the production of new neurons, and promotes the growth of new blood vessels in the brain, thereby improving the brain's ability to function and adapt to new situations.

Facilitation of Thought, Feelings, and Action

The facilitation of thought, feeling, and action in the brain involves complex and interconnected processes within different brain regions.

The prefrontal cortex is the area of the brain responsible for generating thoughts. Higher cognitive functions such as reasoning, problem-solving, decision-making, and planning occur here. Moreover, the prefrontal cortex also regulates emotions and behaviour by modulating activity in other brain regions.

The limbic system, consisting of the amygdala, hippocampus, and hypothalamus, is responsible for generating our emotions. The amygdala processes emotional information and triggers the body's fight or flight response—the hippocampus forms and retrieves memories, including emotional memories. The hypothalamus regulates basic physiological functions such as hunger, thirst, and body temperature. Also, it controls the release of hormones that influence emotions and behaviour.

The motor cortex is responsible for initiating voluntary body movements. It generates actions that control the movement of our body. The motor cortex receives input from other brain regions, including the prefrontal cortex and the basal ganglia, which are involved in the planning and execution of complex motor sequences.

The facilitation of thought, feeling, and action requires coordination between these different brain regions. Communication between neurons occurs through a network of neural pathways that transmit electrical and chemical signals. Neurons that fire together strengthen their connections, forming neural circuits that underlie complex behaviours and mental processes.

Cerebral Vasculature

Like any other organ in the body, the brain also needs a constant and sufficient supply of oxygen and nutrients to function at its best. A complex system of blood vessels and capillaries is responsible for providing the brain with the oxygen-rich blood it requires to perform optimally.

The blood vessels responsible for supplying the brain with oxygenated blood are known as the cerebral vasculature. The network of arteries and veins in the cerebral vasculature actively supplies blood to the brain. These blood vessels are some of the smallest in the body. They are tightly regulated to ensure that the brain receives a constant supply of oxygen and nutrients.

The main arteries that supply blood to the brain are the internal carotid arteries and the vertebral arteries. The carotid arteries are located in the neck and supply blood to the front of the brain, including the frontal, temporal, and parietal lobes. The vertebral arteries supply blood to the back of the brain, even the cerebellum and brainstem. One can locate them at the back of the neck.

The arteries carry blood into the brain, and then the blood is distributed to different regions of the brain through a network of smaller arterioles. Arterioles are some of the smallest blood vessels in the body, with a diameter of fewer than 0.5 millimetres. Yet, despite their small size, arterioles play a crucial role in regulating blood flow to the brain, ensuring that the brain receives a constant supply of oxygen and nutrients.

After passing through the arterioles, the blood enters the capillaries. These are the smallest and the thinnest blood vessels in the body, with a diameter of less than 10 micrometres. Capillaries are responsible for delivering oxygen and nutrients to the brain's cells, as well as removing waste products and carbon dioxide. The capillaries in the brain are different from those found in other parts of the body in that they are tightly regulated and form a barrier known as the blood-brain barrier.

The blood-brain barrier is a protective barrier that helps regulate the exchange of substances between the blood and the brain. Tightly-packed cells create the blood-brain barrier, which prevents large molecules and toxins from entering the brain. This barrier is essential for protecting the brain from harmful substances and maintaining the delicate balance of nutrients and chemicals needed for proper brain function.

Astrocytes surround the brain's capillaries. Astrocytes play a crucial role in regulating blood flow to the brain and maintaining the blood-brain barrier. In addition, these cells help regulate the concentration of chemicals in the brain, ensuring that the brain receives a constant supply of oxygen and nutrients.

The brain also has a unique network of veins known as cerebral veins that drain the blood away from it and back to the heart. The cerebral veins run along the surface of the brain. The cerebral veins drain blood from the capillaries and then converge into more prominent veins known as the dural sinuses. The dural sinuses then drain into the internal jugular veins, which carry blood back to the heart.

The Brain Signalling Network

The communication between cells in the brain is critical for proper brain function, and a cornucopia of different signalling molecules, including hormones and neurotransmitters, mediates this communication. Hormones are signalling molecules produced by specialized cells. They are carried through the bloodstream to act on specific target cells in the body, while neurotransmitters are signalling molecules released by neurons and act on adjacent cells, including other neurons, muscle cells, or glands.

Some of the most well-known neurotransmitters in the brain include serotonin, dopamine, glutamate, NMDA-N-methyl-D-aspartate, and cannabinoids. Each neurotransmitter plays a unique role in mediating communication between cells in the brain.

Serotonin is involved in regulating mood, appetite, and sleep. Cells in the brainstem with specialized functions produce it, and neurons distribute it throughout the brain. Dopamine is another neurotransmitter that is involved in regulating mood, as well as motivation, reward, and movement. Produced by neurons in several regions of the brain, including the substantia nigra and the ventral tegmental area, released in response to rewarding stimuli.

Glutamateisthemostabundantexcitatoryneurotransmitter present in the brain. It involves many functions, including learning and memory, sensory processing, and motor control. Numerous neurons actively produce it in the brain. It acts on several different types of receptors, including the NMDA receptor.

The complexity of the signalling molecules and receptors in the brain underscores the importance of communication between cells in the brain for proper brain function. Disruptions in these signalling pathways can lead to a broad range of neurological and psychiatric disorders, including depression, anxiety, schizophrenia, and Alzheimer's. Understanding the complex interactions between signalling molecules and receptors in the brain is an ongoing area of research, potentially leading to new treatments for these and other disorders.

Brain-derived neurotrophic factor, (BDNF), is also considered the brain fertilizer.

Brain-derived neurotrophic factor is a protein. It ensures the growth, development, and maintenance of neurons in the brain. It is often referred to as a "brain fertilizer" due to its ability to promote the growth and survival of neurons and enhance synaptic plasticity. Synaptic plasticity is the process by which the strength of connections between neurons modify in response to experience. Let's explore the different aspects of BDNF, including its function, regulation, and the role it plays in various neurological and psychiatric disorders.

Function of BDNF

BDNF is produced by many different cells in the brain, including neurons and glial cells. It secretes in the extracellular space and binds to specific receptors on the surface of neurons, which triggers a cascade of intracellular signalling events that promote cell survival, growth, and differentiation.

In the developing brain, BDNF is essential for the formation of new neurons and the proper wiring of neural circuits. One of the key roles of BDNF is to facilitate and promote the growth and survival of neurons during development. Studies have shown that reducing BDNF levels during development can lead to abnormal brain development and cognitive deficits.

BDNF is also important for the maintenance of neurons in the adult brain. It promotes the survival of neurons and enhances their ability to adapt and change in response to experience. Research has revealed that several neurological and psychiatric conditions, including Alzheimer's disease, depression, and schizophrenia, lead to decreased levels of BDNF, which leads to an interest in developing drugs that can increase BDNF levels as a potential treatment for these disorders.

In addition to its role in promoting cell survival and growth, BDNF also plays an important role in enhancing synaptic plasticity. It encourages the growth of new synapses between neurons. It enhances the strength of existing synapses, which are important for learning and memory. Studies have shown that BDNF levels increase during learning and in response to experience, suggesting that it may play a role in the plasticity of neural circuits.

Regulation of BDNF

The regulation of BDNF is a complex process that involves both genetic and environmental factors. Studies have shown a number of different signalling pathways that regulate BDNF expression, including the mitogen-activated protein kinase (MAPK) and phosphatidylinositol 3-kinase (PI3K) pathways.

One of the key regulators of BDNF expression is the transcription factor cAMP response element-binding protein (CREB). CREB binds to specific sites on the BDNF gene and promotes its transcription. Studies have shown that factors that increase the activity of CREB, such as physical exercise and exposure to enriched environments, can increase BDNF expression.

Environmental factors such as stress and diet can also affect BDNF expression. For instance, chronic stress decreases BDNF expression in the hippocampus. This part of the brain is essential for learning and memory. In contrast, diets high in omega-3 fatty acids increase BDNF expression.

Role of BDNF in Neurological and Psychiatric Disorders

ALZHEIMER'S DISEASE

Alzheimer's disease is a neurodegenerative disorder characterized by the progressive loss of neurons and cognitive decline. Studies have shown that BDNF levels are decreased in the brains of Alzheimer's patients, suggesting that BDNF may play a role in the pathogenesis of the disease.

Animal studies have shown that increasing BDNF levels can improve cognitive function and decrease the accumulation of amyloid-beta. Studies suggest that this protein actively contributes to the development of Alzheimer's disease, which has led to an interest in developing drugs that can increase BDNF levels as a potential treatment for the disease.

DEPRESSION

Depression is a highly common psychiatric disorder characterized by feelings of consistent sadness to the extent that it affects routine life and causes a loss of interest in once-enjoyable activities. According to studies, depressed individuals have lower levels of BDNF in their brains, particularly in the hippocampus.

Animal studies have shown that reducing BDNF levels in the hippocampus can lead to depression-like behaviours while increasing BDNF levels can have antidepressant effects; this has led to an interest in developing drugs that can increase BDNF levels as a potential treatment for depression.

SCHIZOPHRENIA

People with schizophrenia experience a variety of symptoms, such as hallucinations, delusions, and cognitive impairments. Studies have shown that individuals with schizophrenia have decreased levels of BDNF in the prefrontal cortex.

Animal studies have shown that increasing BDNF levels in the prefrontal cortex can improve cognitive function and reduce disorder symptoms. It has led to an interest in developing drugs that can increase BDNF levels as a potential treatment for schizophrenia.

POST-TRAUMATIC STRESS DISORDER (PTSD)

PTSD often develops in people who have experienced or witnessed a traumatic event. Studies have shown that individuals with PTSD have decreased levels of BDNF, particularly in the hippocampus.

Animal studies have shown that increasing BDNF levels in the hippocampus can reduce symptoms of PTSD, such as anxiety and fear, which leads to an interest in developing drugs that can increase BDNF levels as a potential treatment for the disorder.

"The food you eat makes up your brain."

The statement "the food you eat makes up your brain" holds a lot of truth when it comes to the relationship between diet and brain health. It is not secret that our diet plays a significant role in our overall health and well-being. However, many people need to recognize its specific impact on the brain. The brain consumes about 20% of the energy from our daily food intake, making it a highly metabolically active organ in the body. Therefore, the quality of our diet directly impacts brain function and development.

Our diet provides the brain with essential nutrients and energy that enable it to perform numerous functions, such as regulating the body's systems, processing sensory information, storing and retrieving memories, and allowing us to learn and think. A balanced diet is needed for the brain to receive all the nutrients it requires for optimal functioning. A diet deficient in essential nutrients may result in impaired cognitive function, poor memory, mood swings, and even depression.

The most important part of the diet is macronutrients, which include carbohydrates, proteins, and fats. These nutrients provide the brain with energy to carry out its functions. The primary energy source for the brain is carbohydrates. Our bodies convert carbohydrates into glucose, the primary fuel for our brain.

Proteins are essential for building and repairing brain tissue and producing neurotransmitters, which are vital for the brain's communication system. Fats, particularly omega-3 fatty acids, are essential for developing and maintaining the brain's cell membranes.

Neurotransmitters are essential chemicals that transmit signals between neurons in the brain. They regulate mood, behaviour, and cognitive function.

Neurotransmitters consist of specific amino acids obtained from food. For example, serotonin requires the amino acid tryptophan, found in protein-rich foods like turkey, chicken, fish, and eggs. Dopamine requires the amino acid tyrosine found in foods like dairy products, eggs, and soy products.

Glial cells are non-neuronal cells in the brain that support and protect neurons. Omega-3 fatty acids are essential for developing and maintaining glial cells. Studies show that omega-3 fatty acids are critical for brain development and can improve cognitive function, memory, and mood.

Brain tissue is composed of various minerals, including zinc, selenium, and magnesium. These minerals are essential for the growth and maintenance of the brain and are involved in many of the brain's functions, such as neurotransmitter production, cell signalling, and energy production. Zinc, for example, is essential for producing enzymes involved in neurotransmitter production and function.

Selenium is essential for the antioxidant defence system, which protects the brain from oxidative stress. Magnesium is involved in energy production and is necessary to maintain healthy brain tissue.

Nerve impulses are the electrical signals that pass between neurons in the brain.

These impulses require B vitamins, such as thiamine, riboflavin, niacin, and pantothenic acid, to function correctly. B vitamins help energy production in the brain and are involved in many of the brain's functions, such as neurotransmitter production and cell signalling.

Serotonin production also requires iron, folate, and vitamin B-12. Iron is necessary for producing haemoglobin, which carries oxygen to the brain. Folate and vitamin B-12 are involved in the synthesis of neurotransmitters, including serotonin. A diet deficient in these nutrients can lead to low serotonin levels, which can result in depression, anxiety, and other mood disorders.

Changing world of Dietary patterns

The world of dietary patterns is constantly evolving, with new research and discoveries changing how we view food and nutrition. New dietary patterns reflecting changes in lifestyle, food availability, and a better understanding of the importance of a balanced diet have replaced the dietary habits of previous generations.

One significant change in recent years is the growing awareness of the impact of food colours and additives on our health. Processed foods often contain high levels of preservatives and other chemicals that have a detrimental effect on our bodies. While these products are readily available, they lack essential nutrients and thus affect our nutritional intake. With the increase in the practice of cooking, buying and eating unhealthy foods, people have ignored the side effects of these chemical-filled foods on health.

Many people are turning to whole foods and natural ingredients to combat this trend, emphasizing consuming more fresh fruits and vegetables, proteins, and healthy fats. These foods are typically rich in essential vitamins and minerals and provide the necessary nutrients to maintain good health and well-being.

The Mediterranean diet is a major example of a dietary pattern rich in nutrients, shown to provide numerous health benefits. This diet emphasizes the consumption of fresh fruits and vegetables, whole grains, and healthy fats such as olive oil. Studies prove that regular consumption of olive oil can prevent depression and is good for heart and brain.

In addition to eat a balanced diet, regular exercise helps maintain physical health and significantly contributes to good mental health. Walking, cycling, and other forms of physical activity can lower stress and anxiety and promote feelings of well-being.

Recent research at the University of Delhi has also highlighted the link between diet quality, nutritional deficiencies, and mental health. The study found that a poor diet can contribute to a range of mental health problems, including depression, anxiety, and cognitive decline.

Conversely, a healthy diet rich in essential nutrients can help protect against these conditions.

It is clear that the world of dietary patterns is changing, with a growing focus on whole foods, natural ingredients, and a balanced diet. By prioritizing our health and well-being and taking steps to ensure that we are getting the nutrients we need, we can help promote a healthier and happier future.

References

1. https://www.health.harvard.edu/mind-and-mood/exercise-is-an-all-natural-treatment-to-fight-depression
2. https://www.ncbi.nlm.nih.gov/pmc/articles/PMC7283326/
3. https://www.thelancet.com/journals/lancet/article/PIIS0140-6736(07)61306-3/fulltext

Reducing or Remitting Depression & Anxiety

Many studies show that dietary changes can help reduce or remit depressive symptoms to even clinical remission. Food, in fact, matters in preventing depression & anxiety but also benefits those who are already suffering.

As we have already established, making lifestyle modifications and simple dietary changes can benefit those with depression to a great extent. Studies suggest that balancing nutrition along with other treatments, such as therapy and antidepressants, can reduce and even remit symptoms of depression, which is true even for severe cases.

Many studies also state that food can not only prevent depression but also benefit those who are already suffering, which happens because, usually, when we are stressed or depressed, we lose our appetite. As a result, our body does not get the required nutrients, starves, and the pre-existing symptoms worsen.

Let us further discuss these nutrients and phytonutrients that help with depression in detail.

OMEGA-3 FATTY ACIDS

Omega-3 fatty acids are vital fats that need to be consumed through diet as our body does not produce them naturally. These fats can be obtained from fish, such as salmon, sardines, and mackerel, and from plant-based sources, including flaxseeds, chia seeds, and walnuts.

Scientific studies have indicated that consuming omega-3 fatty acids can have a favourable impact on mental health by minimizing inflammation in the body and promoting the development of healthy brain cells. Moreover, researches have demonstrated that omega-3 supplements may effectively reduce symptoms of depression, particularly in individuals with high levels of inflammation.

B VITAMINS

B vitamins are important for proper brain functions and the production of neurotransmitters. These vitamins are present in a variety of foods, including whole grains, leafy greens, legumes, and animal products like meat, eggs, and dairy.

Many researches have shown that low levels of certain B vitamins, including folate and vitamin B12, increase the risk of depression and anxiety. One study found that supplementing with folic acid and vitamin B12 reduced depressive symptoms in individuals with depression who were not responding well to medication.

MAGNESIUM

Magnesium is a crucial mineral that performs various bodily functions, such as regulating nerve and muscle activity, producing energy, and synthesizing DNA. Foods that contain magnesium include green leafy vegetables, nuts, seeds, whole grains, and legumes.

Studies have discovered that low levels of magnesium in the body are associated with a higher risk of depression and anxiety. In a research, observations showed that older adults with magnesium deficiency who received magnesium supplementation experienced a reduction in depressive symptoms.

PROBIOTICS

Probiotics are very important for the body and are live bacteria and yeasts that benefit digestive health. These beneficial bacteria are present in fermented foods like yoghurt, kefir, sauerkraut, and kimchi.

Research has shown that probiotics can have a positive impact on mental health by reducing inflammation in the body and improving communication between the gut and the brain. One study found that supplementing with a probiotic containing Lactobacillus and Bifidobacterium reduced symptoms of depression in people with irritable bowel syndrome.

PHYTONUTRIENTS

Researches have shown that certain phytonutrients reduce inflammation in the body, protect the brain from oxidative stress, and improve neurotransmitter function.

Many other ways in which phytonutrients benefit brain health include:

1. Antioxidant properties
2. Neuroprotective effects
3. Improved blood flow to the brain:
4. Anti-inflammatory effects

Here are a few examples of phytonutrients that improve mental health:

1. **Curcumin:** Curcumin is the active ingredient in the daily household spice, turmeric, used in Indian cuisine. Research has shown that curcumin has anti-inflammatory and antioxidant properties and may have a positive impact on mental health. One study found that supplementing with curcumin reduced symptoms of depression in individuals with major depressive disorder.

2. **Flavonoids:** Flavonoids are a type of phytonutrient found in fruits, vegetables, tea and dark chocolate. Researches have shown that flavonoids may have anti-inflammatory and antioxidant properties and a positive impact on mental health. One study found that consuming a flavonoid-rich cocoa drink improved mood and cognitive performance in healthy adults.
3. **Anthocyanins:** Anthocyanins are a type of flavonoid found in dark-coloured fruits and vegetables like blueberries, blackberries, and eggplant. Researches have shown that anthocyanins may have anti-inflammatory and antioxidant properties and may have a positive impact on mental health. One study found that consuming a blueberry drink improved mood and cognitive function in children.

To ensure that you are getting enough phytonutrients and essential nutrients in your diet, regularly consume a wide variety of fresh vegetables, legumes, grains, nuts, and other plant-based foods.

References

1. https://www.healthline.com/health/phytonutrients
2. https://www.psychologytoday.com/us/blog/cravings/202205/4-important-phytonutrients-brain-health
3. https://pubmed.ncbi.nlm.nih.gov/30551400/https://pubmed.ncbi.nlm.nih.gov/30551400/

Folate

WHAT IS FOLATE?

Folate is a naturally occurring vitamin B found in various green leafy vegetables and other foods. It is a water-soluble vitamin which is easily absorbed in the body through food. Sometimes, it is separately added to foods, known as fortified foods, and sold as a supplement in the form of folic acid.

HEALTH BENEFITS OF FOLATE

Folate is necessary to perform most bodily functions on a daily basis. Discussed below are some of its most important health benefits.

- **Decreases the risk of cancer:** A study in 2018 suggests that folate deficiency may elevate the risk of developing cancer. Thus, consuming the required amount of folate can keep you safe from this disease.
- **Healthy Pregnancy:** When taken during pregnancy, folate prevents neural tube defects, which means that the neural tube comprising the brain and spinal cord closes incompletely. This can result in spina bifida or anencephaly in the developing foetus. Lower levels of folate and vitamin B12 often result in these conditions.
- **Lowers blood pressure:** In a 20-year follow-up study by Pengcheng Xun et al., it was found that increased folic intake reduces blood pressure and the risk of developing cardiovascular diseases later in life.
- **Reduces risk of age-related macular degeneration:** Age-related macular degeneration is nothing but an eye disorder that affects central vision. The exact cause of this disease is not known. However, inflammation, oxidative stress and elevated levels of homocysteine might play a role.

A randomized trial by William Christen recommends consuming 2500 mcg of folic acid every day to lower the chances of age-related macular degeneration by about 40%.

ROLE OF FOLATE IN BRAIN HEALTH

For optimum growth and development, eat the right matters. This is because a growing body has high nutritional needs to carry out simple processes and energy transfer among cells.

This is true not only for pregnant and lactating mothers but also for children in their growth phase and the elderly to maintain good health.

The brain especially needs nutrients since it runs the most complex processes of the body. They help metabolize C1 and form neurotransmitters. A growing body requires folate and other B vitamins for brain health across all age groups. In addition, evidence suggests that maternal folate status throughout pregnancy is important for the neurodevelopment and behaviour of the baby.

Furthermore, folate improves cognition as an individual becomes older.

According to a recent clinical trial, subjects who were given folic acid supplements and vitamin B over a two-year period showed reduced brain atrophy in older age.

SOURCES OF FOLATE AND THE RIGHT WAYS TO CONSUME IT

Folate is abundant in a wide variety of foods, such as dark green leafy veggies, beans, edible seeds and others. However, if the nutritional demand of the individual is high, it is essential to take supplements. Folic acid is better absorbed in the body than folate; hence, it is added excessively to processed foods and supplements.

Some of the most important sources of folate include:

- Peanuts, kidney beans and black-eyed peas
- Beans
- Dark green leafy vegetables such as spinach, asparagus, sprouts, broccoli, lettuce, and others.
- Fresh fruits
- Whole grains
- Beef liver
- Eggs

- Seafood
- Sunflower seeds
- Fortified foods and supplements

The availability of folate in food depends on how it is cooked or processed. When cooked covered, it may evaporate. On the other hand, cooking for a longer duration destroys the folic acid in the food. Furthermore, the rate of absorption differs in every individual. Thus, it is not possible to measure how much folic acid a person receives through a certain amount of food intake.

RDA or Recommended Dietary Allowance

The recommended dietary allowance for folate is about 400 mcg for men and women above 19 years. Pregnant women, lactating mothers and alcoholics require about 500-600 mcg of folate.

The tolerable upper intake level of folate is about 1000 mcg. This means that folic acid should be taken at most 1000 mcg in a day to avoid its toxic effects.

References:

1. https://www.ncbi.nlm.nih.gov/pmc/articles/PMC1810582/
2. https://www.hsph.harvard.edu/nutritionsource/folic-acid/
3. https://www.psychiatrist.com/jcp/depression/folate-depression-efficacy-safety-differences-formulations/

Iron

WHAT IS IRON?

Iron is an essential mineral for the body to perform vital functions and promote growth and development. It is a part of haemoglobin that carries oxygenated blood from the lungs to different parts of the body. More than that, it allows the muscles to store and utilize oxygen as and when needed. It is also a part of other body processes. Therefore, its disruption affects most physiological functions of the body, including the brain processes.

Our body is not capable of forming its own Iron, so it should be consumed through food. If the body does not have sufficient Iron for its needs, iron deficiency or anaemia sets in. Anaemia is a condition characterized by the lack of healthy red blood cells.

This results in a lot of complications and requires immediate care. People with highly deficient Iron may require additional iron supplements to compensate for the deficiency since food may not be enough.

ROLE OF IRON IN BRAIN HEALTH

As already established, Iron is an important component in running day-to-day body processes, especially the brain. Therefore, when its levels in the body are disturbed, brain health is significantly affected.

Let us understand how brain health is affected by iron levels in the body.

Researches suggest that inadequate and excessive iron levels directly affect cognition and behaviour. This is because Iron is particularly responsible for maintaining the high metabolic and energy needs of the brain tissues. As a result, the body, especially the brain, requires considerable amounts of Iron during periods of rapid growth.

Iron is mainly sourced from the blood in the body throughout life and is variably distributed throughout the brain. If iron level is low, the brain gets lesser amount of Iron, directly affecting brain function.

Iron deficiency, in fact, impacts motor function, social behaviour, and cognition.

On the other hand, iron accumulation in the brain shows links to ageing, neurodegenerative disorders, and psychosocial disorders. Studies of these effects on animals showed evident behavioural dysfunctions and neurological disturbances. These effects may be present due to disturbances in other nutrients as well. It is thus essential to maintain a healthy nutrient intake for overall health benefits.

The brain processes in which Iron plays a vital role include:

- Regulation of axon myelination, which is a nerve fibre of the brain
- Neural transmission
- Synaptic function, which means the regulation of brain signals
- Impaired cognitive behaviour
- Altered social behaviour
- Iron is a part of the structure of many enzymes and proteins that regulate energy metabolism.
- Iron is a cofactor which ensures the proper functioning of neuro developmental mechanisms.
- It plays a role in the formation of dopamine and serotonin, which is a "happy hormone" responsible for feeling elated.
- It balances the signals of mood function in the brain.
- Iron also interacts with various other metals, such as Zinc, in performing brain processes.

HEALTH BENEFITS OF IRON

Doctors often prescribe Iron supplements when dietary forms of Iron are inadequate to meet the body's demands or the deficiency is so high that immediate use of Iron is warranted. However, it is always advisable to consume Iron through natural food sources rather than swallowing pills.

Moreover, you should also identify and eliminate factors that affect iron absorption and focus on consuming Iron through foods. This is because many iron-rich foods have other beneficial effects on the body and support overall health.

HEALTHY PREGNANCY

During pregnancy, there is an increased need for increased blood production. This occurs to provide the developing foetus with oxygen and nutrients; consequently, the need for iron increases. At this time, the body tries to absorb maximum Iron.

Insufficient iron intake or other factors that cause inadequate absorption can lead to iron deficiency and require outsourcing for maintaining optimum mother-baby health. If the body does not have sufficient Iron, it may lead to low birth weight and premature birth. In addition, it may cause low iron reserves and impaired cognitive and behavioural development in children. Thus, it is very important for pregnant women to meet the nutritional demands of the body.

Pregnant women with Iron deficiency may also be prone to infections since Iron plays a role in supporting the immune system.

ENERGY

Iron plays a role in carrying oxygen from the lungs to the muscles, brain, and other parts along with haemoglobin, and thus, is a crucial nutrient for mental and physical well-being. Insufficient iron intake may disrupt processes that are responsible for energy production. Iron deficiency often results in increased irritability, decreased stamina and lack of focus.

BETTER ATHLETIC PERFORMANCE

Iron deficiency is more common among young female athletes than in people with an inactive lifestyle. Men may also be affected, but studies have found that female endurance athletes like long-distance runners are most prone to iron deficiency. Doctors, therefore, recommend taking an additional 10 mg of Iron per day to the current RDA for iron intake.

Iron deficiency in athletes greatly disturbs athletic performance and also weakens immunity. In addition, the lack of haemoglobin reduces performance during physical exertion due to an inadequate supply of oxygen to the body's muscles.

FOOD SOURCES AND HOW TO CONSUME IT/RDA

The amount of Iron needed each day depends on multiple factors such as age, sex, the kind of diet consumed, and the extent of physical activities. Children often need about 8-15 mg of Iron, while adults require 12-20mg of Iron daily. Vegetarians often require additional iron intake since they do not eat poultry, meat, or seafood.

Different foods that contain natural Iron include lean meat, poultry, seafood, white beans, spinach, lentils, kidney beans, peas, nuts, dried fruits like raisins, and fortified cereals and bread. These foods are easily available in the market and can be consumed raw or after cooking with the lid covered. The lid prevents nutrients from escaping in the form of steam.

Other supplements that contain Iron are multivitamins and only iron supplements. These pills contain Iron in the form of ferrous sulphate, ferrous citrate, ferric gluconate, or ferric sulphate. Supplements are meant only for adults; children should not consume these supplements without professional supervision. This is because excessive Iron has detrimental effects on the growth and development of children.

Moreover, many reported cases of an accidental overdose of Iron, the leading cause of fatal poisoning in kids under the age of 6 years. Thus, it is advisable to consult the doctor before starting any supplements.

References

1. https://medlineplus.gov/iron.html
2. https://timesofindia.indiatimes.com/life-style/health-fitness/diet/feeling-depressed-lately-iron-deficiency-may-trigger-gloomy-emotions-too/photostory/96429609.cms
3. https://www.ncbi.nlm.nih.gov/pmc/articles/PMC6789770/
4. https://www.medicalnewstoday.com/articles/anemia-and-depression
5. https://www.thecaregrouppc.com/low-iron-depression-and-anxiety/
6. https://psychcentral.com/depression/anemia-and-depression

Omega-3

WHAT IS OMEGA-3?

Omega-3 is a type of poly unsaturated fatty acid that is essential for human health. There are several different types of omega-3 fatty acids, including eicosapentaenoic acid (EPA), docosahexaenoic acid (DHA), and alpha-linolenic acid (ALA).

EPA and DHA are abundant in oily fishes like sardine, salmon, and mackeral. In contrast, ALA is present in some plant-based sources such as flaxseeds, chia seeds, and walnuts.

Omega-3 fatty acids are important for maintaining brain function, supporting cardiovascular health, and reducing inflammation in the body. Research has also suggested that omega-3s may have a positive effect on mood, cognition, and overall well-being.

HEALTH BENEFITS OF OMEGA-3

Omega-3 fatty acids are essential nutrients that maintain overall health and well-being. These healthy fats play a crucial role in the functioning of the body. They are involved in several vital processes, including brain function, heart health, and reducing inflammation. Some of its important health benefits include:

- **Heart Health:** Omega-3 fatty acids are also important for maintaining a healthy heart.There are many researches that have shown that omega-3s can help lower triglyceride levels, reduce blood pressure, and improve overall heart health. Additionally, omega-3s may help reduce the risk of heart disease and stroke. They may even help prevent the formation of blood clots.
- **Joint Health:** Omega-3 fatty acids have anti-inflammatory properties, which make them beneficial for joint health. Researches have shown that omega-3s might lower joint pain and stiffness in individuals with rheumatoid arthritis, osteoarthritis, and other inflammatory joint conditions. Additionally, omega-3s help improve joint mobility and reduce the need for pain medication.
- **Eye Health:** Omega-3 fatty acids are important for maintaining proper eye health and vision. Researches have shown that omega-3s may help lower the risk of age-related macular degeneration. DHA, one of the primary types of omega-3s, is a major component of the retina and is essential for maintaining proper vision.
- **Mental Health:** Omega-3 fatty acids may also be beneficial for mental health. Many studies have shown that omega-3s may help improve symptoms of depression and other mood disorders. Additionally, omega-3s may help reduce the risk of developing schizophrenia and other psychotic disorders.
- **Pregnancy and Early Childhood Development:** Omega-3 fatty acids are essential for proper foetal and early childhood development. DHA, one of the primary types of omega-3s, is essential for the development of brain and nervous system in infants and young children. Researches

have shown that omega-3 supplementation during pregnancy and breastfeeding may help improve cognitive development, lower the chances of preterm birth, and improve the overall health of both mother and child.

- **Cancer Prevention:** Omega-3 fatty acids may also help reduce the risk of certain types of cancer. Researches have shown that omega-3s may help reduce the risk of breast, prostate, and colon cancer. In addition, omega-3s may help reduce the risk of developing leukaemia and other types of blood cancers.

ROLE OF OMEGA-3 IN BRAIN HEALTH

Omega-3 fatty acids, particularly docosahexaenoic acid (DHA), play a vital role in brain health and cognitive function. DHA is a key component of brain tissue and is necessary for the proper development and function of brain cells. Studies have shown that omega-3s may help improve memory, mood, and cognitive function and may even lower the chances of developing Alzheimer's disease and other forms of dementia.

Some other brain health benefits of omega-3 are:

- **Brain Development:** The brain and nervous system require Omega-3 fatty acids for development in infants and young children, with DHA being especially essential. Studies indicate that supplementing with omega-3 during pregnancy and breastfeeding can improve cognitive development, decrease the likelihood of premature birth, and enhance the health of both mother and child.
- **Improving Cognitive Function:** Omega-3s help improve cognitive function in people of all ages. Many researches have proved that omega-3 supplementation may help improve memory, attention, and processing speed, particularly in older adults. Additionally, omega-3s may help reduce the risk of cognitive decline. They may even improve symptoms of Alzheimer's disease and other types of dementia.

- **Reducing Inflammation:** Omega-3s have anti-inflammatory properties and may help reduce inflammation in the brain. Inflammation causes the development of neurological and psychiatric disorders, including depression, anxiety, and schizophrenia. Research has shown that omega-3 supplementation may help reduce symptoms of depression and anxiety and may even improve symptoms in people with schizophrenia.
- **Neuroplasticity:** Neuroplasticity refers to the brain's ability to change and adapt over time. Omega-3s may help support neuroplasticity by promoting the growth and development of new brain cells and connections. Omega-3 supplementation may help improve brain function and cognitive performance in people of all ages.
- **Protecting Against Age-Related Decline:** Age-related cognitive decline is a natural part of the ageing process, but omega-3s may help slow down this decline. Researches have shown that omega-3 supplementation may help improve cognitive function in older adults and may even reduce the risk of developing Alzheimer's disease and other forms of dementia.

FOOD SOURCES OF OMEGA-3 AND THE WAY TO CONSUME IT

Our body does not produce Omega-3 fatty acids. Hence, they must be outsourced through food or supplements. Some of the most common food sources of omega-3 are:

- **Fatty Fish:** Fatty fish are the best dietary source of omega-3s.
- **Nuts and Seeds:** Flaxseeds, chia seeds, hemp seeds, and walnuts are good sources.
- Plant Oils: Certain plant oils are also a good source of omega-3s, such as canola, soybean and flaxseed oil.
- **Supplements**

RECOMMENDED DIETARY ALLOWANCE

For omega-3 fatty acids, the RDA varies depending on the specific type of omega-3. The RDA for alpha-linolenic acid (ALA), found in plant-based foods, is 1.6 grams per day for adult males and 1.1 grams per day for adult females. The RDA for eicosapentaenoic acid (EPA) and docosahexaenoic acid (DHA) found in fatty fish and fish oil supplements is currently under review. Still, the current adequate intake (AI) for adults is 250-500 milligrams per day.

References

1. https://ods.od.nih.gov/factsheets/Omega3FattyAcids-HealthProfessional/
2. https://www.health.harvard.edu/blog/omega-3-fatty-acids-for-mood-disorders-2018080314414
3. https://www.ncbi.nlm.nih.gov/books/NBK537084/

Magnesium

WHAT IS MAGNESIUM?

Magnesium is an essential mineral in the body, often obtained through food and supplements. It helps maintain the normal bone structure, and if deficient, it may lead to diseases such as osteoporosis, clogged arteries, heart ailments, high blood pressure, diabetes, and stroke.

Magnesium is an essential nutrient for the body since it is involved in more than 320 enzyme reactions occurring in the body. It regulates muscle and nerve function and blood pressure and supports the immune system.

The skeletal tissues in our bodies store most of the magnesium. In contrast, the soft tissues, muscles, and fluids in the body store the remaining. An adult has about 25 gm of magnesium stored in the body.

If you don't have enough magnesium taken through diet, you may experience deficiency symptoms. Magnesium deficiency can lead to many complications, such as convulsions, fatigue, muscle weakness, abnormal eye movements, etc.

HEALTH BENEFITS OF MAGNESIUM

Magnesium is one of the most essential macrominerals. Consumption of these major minerals should be in large quantities regularly. At least 100 mg of magnesium is required on a daily basis to keep bodily processes in homeostasis. Getting enough magnesium can prevent or treat various chronic diseases such as Alzheimer's disease, cardiovascular diseases, type 2 diabetes, and migraine.

Let us discuss the role of magnesium in maintaining optimal health:

- **Bone health:** Not only is calcium necessary to maintain bone health, but it also requires adequate magnesium levels for bone formation. A study in 2013 associated adequate magnesium intake with improved bone crystal formation, increased bone density, and a decreased risk of osteoporosis in females in the postmenopausal phase.

  Magnesium improves bone health by regulating calcium and vitamin D levels, another two nutrients vital for maintaining bone health.

- **Diabetes:** Researches suggest that people who consume a diet rich in magnesium carry a reduced risk of developing type 2 diabetes. This may be because magnesium helps regulate glucose and insulin metabolism.

  A 2015 review in the World Journal of Diabetes states that most people with diabetes have low magnesium levels.

  A magnesium deficiency may worsen insulin resistance, which is a condition that often develops before type 2 diabetes. On the other hand, insulin resistance may cause low magnesium levels.

- **Cardiovascular health:** The role of magnesium in maintaining heart health is well-known. Research has found that magnesium keeps heart muscles healthy.

  A 2018 review states that magnesium deficiency increases the risk of developing cardiovascular diseases. The study also concluded that people with congestive heart failure and other cardiovascular diseases had lower levels of magnesium than normal people. Moreover, its deficiency can worsen heart conditions. This important essential mineral works at a cellular level and, thus, is highly crucial for maintaining heart health.

- **Migraine headaches:** Therapy with magnesium may reduce or prevent episodes of migraine headaches. This is because the deficiency of magnesium affects neurotransmitters' function and limits the constriction of the blood vessels. Both these factors are directly responsible for causing migraine headaches.

- **Premenstrual syndrome:** Magnesium may also play a role in premenstrual syndrome (PMS).

  Small-scale studies, including a 2012 article, suggest that taking magnesium supplements along with vitamin B-6 can improve PMS symptoms. However, a more recent 2019 review reports that the research is mixed and further studies are needed to prove this.

ROLE OF MAGNESIUM IN BRAIN HEALTH

Magnesium plays a key role in regulating the functions of N-methyl-D-aspartate (NMDA) glutamate receptors in the brain, which are important for learning and memory.

Glutamate is a neurotransmitter. It stimulates brain activity, but excessive amounts can lead to overstimulation of cells and cell death. This overexcitation links to a variety of neurological conditions, such as Parkinson's, multiple sclerosis, and Alzheimer's, as well as depression and anxiety.

Magnesium works to block the actions of glutamate in the NMDA receptors. When magnesium levels are low, fewer NMDA receptors are blocked, leading to overstimulation and cell damage. This suggests that magnesium could be beneficial in preventing and treating depression.

RESEARCH ON MAGNESIUM FOR DEPRESSION

Although there is promise in the use of dietary magnesium for depression, the exact effects are not yet fully understood. However, some research has suggested that magnesium supplementation may be beneficial for depression:

One study in 2015 discovered a significant link between depression in adults and low magnesium intake. In 2017, a randomized clinical trial published in the journal PLoS One found that taking magnesium chloride supplements led to noticeable improvements in depressive symptoms.

The study also revealed that those who took antidepressants experienced more significant benefits when taking magnesium, suggesting that it may be useful in combination with antidepressant medication.

FOOD SOURCES AND HOW TO CONSUME IT/RDA

In general, the rich sources of magnesium are nuts, seeds, greens, dry beans, wheat germ, wheat bran, whole grains, and oat bran. The recommended dietary allowance for adult men is about 400-420 mg per day, whereas for adult women is approximately 310-320 mg per day.

References

1. https://my.clevelandclinic.org/health/articles/15650-magnesium-rich-food
2. https://www.medicalnewstoday.com/articles/286839#_noHeaderPrefixedContent
3. https://www.healthline.com/nutrition/magnesium-benefits#TOC_TITLE_HDR_4

4. https://www.verywellmind.com/magnesium-for-depression-does-it-help-5112650

Potassium and Depression

WHAT IS POTASSIUM?

Potassium is an essential mineral or an electrolyte found naturally in foods. It is known as an electrolyte since it carries a small amount of electrical charge, which activates cell and nerve functions.

One of the most significant benefits of potassium is its ability to boost your mental health and alleviate symptoms of depression.

It is a crucial electrolyte that helps regulate nerve and muscle function in your body. This includes the nerve and muscle cells in your brain, which play a critical role in your mental health. When your body is deficient in potassium, it can lead to symptoms of depression, anxiety, and other mental health disorders.

HEALTH BENEFITS OF POTASSIUM

Potassium is an essential mineral necessary for performing the basic functions of the human body. Below are some of the health advantages that potassium provides:

1. **Regulates blood pressure:** Potassium helps regulate blood pressure by counteracting the effects of sodium. It helps reduce the risk of hypertension and stroke.
2. **Supports heart health:** Potassium helps maintain the normal heart rhythm and prevent irregular heartbeat. It also helps reduce the risk of heart disease.
3. **Supports muscle function:** Potassium is necessary for proper muscle function, such as contraction and relaxation. It helps prevent muscle cramps, weakness, and fatigue.
4. **Maintains bone health:** Potassium helps maintain bone health by reducing the risk of osteoporosis and bone loss.

5. **Improves kidney function:** Potassium helps improve kidney function by promoting the elimination of waste products from the body.
6. **Regulates fluid balance:** Potassium helps regulate fluid balance in the body. It helps maintain proper hydration and prevent dehydration.
7. **Reduces the risk of stroke:** Potassium reduces the risk of stroke by lowering the risk of hypertension. In addition, it improves the blood flow to the brain.
8. **Improves digestion:** Potassium improves digestion by regulating food movement through the digestive tract.

ROLE OF POTASSIUM IN BRAIN HEALTH

Potassium is a vital mineral that performs many bodily functions, such as maintaining proper brain function. It is an electrolyte that regulates the balance of fluids in the body, especially in the brain. The brain requires a consistent supply of oxygen and nutrients to function properly, and potassium is essential for regulating blood flow to the brain and ensuring that the brain receives an adequate supply of nutrients.

Potassium also helps support nerve function and communication between brain cells. It is involved in transmitting electrical impulses in the brain, which is critical for many aspects of brain function, such as learning, memory, and attention.

Studies have also suggested that potassium plays a vital role in protecting against age-related cognitive decline and reducing the risk of stroke. Low potassium levels link to an increased risk of stroke, and increasing potassium intake has a protective effect.

FOOD SOURCES AND HOW TO CONSUME IT/RDA

Good dietary sources of potassium include:

1. **Fruits:** bananas, oranges, cantaloupe, honeydew melon, apricots, prunes, and raisins.
2. **Vegetables:** leafy greens like spinach, fenugreek and kale, broccoli, potatoes, sweet potatoes, squash, tomatoes, and avocados.
3. **Beans and Legumes:** kidney beans, chickpeas, lentils, soybeans, and lima beans.
4. **Nuts and Seeds:** almonds, pistachios, sunflower seeds, and pumpkin seeds.
5. **Dairy products:** milk and yoghurt.

The recommended daily allowance for potassium is about 2,500 milligrams per day for adults. However, this can vary depending on factors such as age, sex, and medical conditions. Discuss with your doctor to determine your specific potassium needs.

RELATED RESEARCH LINKING POTASSIUM AND DEPRESSION

Potassium is necessary for various physiological functions, including proper brain function. Researches have linked low potassium levels to various mental health conditions, including depression. Let's discuss the relationship between potassium and depression, including the latest researches on the same.

In addition to its potential role in depression, potassium has links with other mental health conditions as well. Researches have suggested that low potassium levels may increase the risk of bipolar disorder, a mental health disorder characterized by extreme mood swings. One study found that individuals with bipolar disorder had lower levels of potassium in their blood than healthy individuals.

Researches have also linked low potassium levels to anxiety, characterized by excessive worry and fear. Low potassium levels are associated with higher levels of anxiety in women.

References

1. https://ods.od.nih.gov/factsheets/Potassium-HealthProfessional/
2. https://www.mayoclinic.org/diseases-conditions/rumination-syndrome/care-at-mayo-clinic/mac-20377339
3. https://www.health.harvard.edu/staying-healthy/potassium-the-silent-helper
4. https://medlineplus.gov/ency/article/000479.htm

Selenium

WHAT IS SELENIUM?

A trace mineral known as Selenium is important for performing basic physiological functions in the body. For example, it plays a role in improving cognitive abilities and enhances immunity and fertility. In addition, it maintains thyroid hormone metabolism and DNA synthesis. Furthermore, it protects the body from oxidative damage and various infections by strengthening the body's natural defence mechanism.

The amount of Selenium that food contains depends on the concentration of soil and water where it is grown. This Selenium gets stored in the body after being taken through food in the skeletal tissues. Some food sources include seafood, meats and Brazil nuts.

Selenium can not only be taken through food but also through supplements if it is deficient.

HEALTH BENEFITS OF SELENIUM

The actual impact of Selenium on the body needs more understanding. However, it does benefit overall health, including heart health, skeletal system, brain health and immune system. Let's discuss these aspects in detail.

CARDIOVASCULAR SYSTEM

As per the ODS, selenoproteins influence heart health by preventing the oxidative modifications of body fats. As a result, inflammation reduces as platelets build up. However, there is not enough clinical evidence that suggests Selenium lowers the risk of cardiovascular diseases.

COGNITIVE HEALTH BENEFITS

Selenium is known for its antioxidant properties that reduce the risk of brain disorders. Regular intake of Selenium can delay the Age-related cognitive decline and brain impairments that occur due to Alzheimer's disease.

THYROID-RELATED DISORDERS

Selenium is known to maintain thyroid function. The International Journal of Endocrinology has published studies that support the role of Selenium in treating and maintaining thyroid-related disorders. In addition, they have also documented details about how Selenium can prevent the onset of thyroid diseases, especially in females. However, there is a need for more research to make it a full-fledged treatment supplement.

CANCER

Selenium plays a role in the repair of DNA, making it a potential cancer prevention tool. However, the type of cancer and Selenium are big factors to consider, according to a 2016 study. Another 2018 review suggests that selenium supplements may not be so helpful in preventing cancer.

ROLE OF SELENIUM IN BRAIN HEALTH

Researchers have conducted several experiments to assess the role of Selenium in brain health. They have found altered levels of this vital mineral in the brain and blood of people with dementia using biomarkers. Altered levels may be due to disease-related processes or disrupted nutritional patterns. Other reasons may be the inability of the body to utilize the available Selenium in the body effectively.

Another study revealed that cognitive decline could be stabilized with high doses of Selenium, even though there was a risk of side effects in a few participants.

Yet another study found the benefits in people with cognitive decline when provided with a combination of probiotics and Selenium. However, they did not find much difference with Selenium only.

FOOD SOURCES OF SELENIUM

Some of the good sources of Selenium are listed below. You can add these to your diet based on your preference and liking.

- Brazil nuts
- Tuna
- Baked halibut
- Cooked brown rice
- Egg
- White bread

The recommended dietary allowance of Selenium on a daily basis is about 55 mcg for most adults. However, the number is slightly higher during growth phases such as pregnancy and lactation, and teenagers.

References

1. https://ods.od.nih.gov/factsheets/Selenium-HealthProfessional/
2. https://www.ncbi.nlm.nih.gov/pmc/articles/PMC7982578/ https://www.ncbi.nlm.nih.gov/pmc/articles/PMC7982578/
3. https://www.ncbi.nlm.nih.gov/pmc/articles/PMC7982578/
4. https://www.alzdiscovery.org/cognitive-vitality/ratings/selenium

Thiamine

WHAT IS THIAMINE?

Thiamine is a water-soluble vitamin B1, found naturally in foods. Some food products contain it, while others sell it as a dietary supplement.

Multivitamins commonly contain Thiamine; it can be taken as a separate supplement or along with other B complex vitamins. Our body needs Thiamine to promote growth and development and to perform essential cellular functions.

Doctors use it to treat Beriberi, nerve disorders, and Wernicke-Korsakoff syndrome. Recent studies have shown that it improves symptoms of depression.

Foods that are rich sources of Thiamine include brown rice, pork, nuts, poultry, whole grains, beans, peas, and fortified foods such as cereals, bread, and instant formulas. In addition to natural foods, if you take supplements, multivitamin pills can provide you with 1.5 mg of Thiamine.

HEALTH BENEFITS OF THIAMINE

Vitamin B1 is an essential vitamin needed by the body for day-to-day functioning. But how does its intake benefit the body? Let us discuss that.

Thiamine is known to prevent medical complications related to the nervous system, muscles, brain, heart, intestines and stomach. It aids in the process of electrolyte flow in and out of the nerve and muscle cells. Moreover, it also prevents Beriberi, a disorder of the nerves, heart and digestive system.

TREATMENT OF MEDICAL CONDITIONS

Treatment with Thiamine helps treat peripheral neuritis. Inflammation of nerves other than the brain characterizes this condition.

Moreover, it helps treat ulcerative colitis, people with lack of nutrition, persistent diarrhoea, and even people in coma to meet their nutritional demands for survival.

Furthermore, even athletes take Thiamine to enhance their performance on the field since it is not a prohibited substance.

DIABETES AND CARDIOVASCULAR DISEASES

Studies show that Thiamine reduces elevated blood sugar and insulin levels. As already discussed, it combines with sugar to produce instant energy. Moreover, it also lowers high blood pressure when taken regularly.

Long-term and regular intake of vitamin B1 prevents heart-related complications and keeps cardiovascular health in check.

When the body has optimum levels of vitamin B1, it minimizes the risk of heart diseases. This is because it plays a role in the production of acetylcholine, an important messenger that transmits information between the nerves and muscles. In the absence of acetylcholine, the heart wouldn't be able to perform its functions. Hence, vitamin B1 deficiency can lead to uneven cardiac function.

ENERGY PRODUCTION

On interacting with sugars in the body, Thiamine converts into energy and becomes readily available for use. In addition, it hastens the process while supporting other enzymes involved in the reaction.

INFECTION

This vitamin lowers the effects of sepsis in the body. Sepsis is the severe response of the body to an infection, which can be fatal if not treated on time. Low levels of Thiamine also increase the risk of fatality during sepsis. A combination of vitamins B1 and C helps control symptoms of sepsis.

During sepsis, the kidneys may also get infected. Thiamine reduces and prevents the chances of renal failure under such conditions.

ROLE OF THIAMINE IN BRAIN HEALTH

Vitamin B1 plays a crucial role in maintaining brain function. Its deficiency may significantly affect specific brain processes and may lead to severe conditions such as Alzheimer's disease and Wernicke-Korsakoff syndrome.

The cause of its deficiency is usually due to severe malnutrition, HIV-AIDS, chronic alcoholism and gastrointestinal diseases.

ALZHEIMER'S DISEASE

Lack of vitamin B1 can lead to dementia in Wernicke-Korsakoff syndrome. Thus, researchers speculate that Thiamine may be able to help improve symptoms of Alzheimer's.

When administered in patients with Alzheimer's, Thiamine improves their cognitive function. However, the absorption of this vitamin is poor in elderly people. For using Thiamine as a full-fledged treatment option for Alzheimer's, there is a need for research.

WERNICKE-KORSAKOFF SYNDROME

This is a brain disorder, which may be of two types depending on the nerves involved - peripheral or central nervous systems. This disease is common among chronic alcoholics with malnutrition. Memory issues and nerve damage characterize it. Thiamine may help improve muscle coordination and confusion in affected people; rarely does it improve memory loss.

DEPRESSION

Vitamin B1 supplements enhance the effects of antidepressants. This is because people with depression often experience a loss of appetite. When this happens, the unfulfilled nutrient demand of the body results in functional imbalance.

With time, the symptoms of depression worsen. So when you seek treatment, professionals often prescribe antidepressants along with multivitamins that compensate for the lack of nutrition, thus restoring the harmony of the body's physiological functions.

Consequently, your mood stabilizes, and symptoms of depression wean off.

MEMORY ENHANCEMENT

Getting enough Thiamine can improve your memory to a great extent. It is especially useful in the older people who lose memory due to age-related factors or dementia. This vitamin also enhances focus and concentration. In addition, it has a positive effect on the brain and is known as a 'morale vitamin'.

FOOD SOURCES AND HOW TO CONSUME IT/RDA

The outer layers and the germ of cereals, yeast, nuts, pork, beef, pulses and whole grains find higher concentrations of vitamin B1. Cauliflower, potatoes, asparagus, oranges, and kale are some of the fruits and vegetables with a high concentration of Thiamine. This essential nutrient is also present in the liver, eggs, and blackstrap molasses.

We should consume Thiamine regularly as our bodies do not store Thiamine. The recommended dietary allowance means the amount of Thiamine one should consume every day in order to meet the body's requirements. Normally, adults need about 1-1.2 mg of Thiamine. However, pregnant women and lactating mothers require larger amounts; hence, the amount of required RDA is 1.4 mg daily. For children, it is better to consult doctors to understand their dietary needs based on age and physical activities.

References

1. https://www.webmd.com/vitamins/ai/ingredientmono-965/thiamine-vitamin-b1
2. https://www.ncbi.nlm.nih.gov/books/NBK482360/
3. https://www.medicalnewstoday.com/articles/219545
4. https://www.healthline.com/nutrition/thiamine-deficiency-symptoms
5. https://ods.od.nih.gov/factsheets/Thiamin-HealthProfessional/

Vitamin C

WHAT IS VITAMIN C?

Vitamin C is necessary for repairing and developing tissues in the body. It is also known to be an effective antioxidant that shields the body from harmful free radicals.

Collagen is a vital protein for maintaining healthy skin, connective tissues, and bones, and Vitamin C plays a significant role in its production. Additionally, Vitamin C can enhance the immune system, assist with iron absorption from plant sources, and facilitate the healing of wounds.

While the body is not able to produce vitamin C on its own, it can be obtained through a variety of foods such as citrus fruits, berries, kiwi, papaya, broccoli, bell peppers, and spinach. Vitamin C supplements can also help treat certain health conditions or support overall health and well-being.

HEALTH BENEFITS OF VITAMIN C

Ascorbic acid, or vitamin C, is a potent antioxidant with multiple advantages for our health. Being a water-soluble vitamin, it is necessary for the growth and healing of body tissues. The following are some health benefits associated with vitamin C:

1. **Boosts the immune system:** Vitamin C plays an essential role in the immune system by stimulating the production of white blood cells. As a result, it helps fight infections and diseases in the body. It also helps protect the immune cells from damage caused by free radicals.
2. **Protects against chronic diseases:** Vitamin C is a powerful antioxidant that shields the body from the detrimental effects of free radicals. These free radicals are responsible for causing chronic ailments like diabetes, heart disease, and cancer.
3. **Improves skin health:** Vitamin C is essential in the creation of collagen, which is a protein vital for maintaining healthy skin, hair, and nails. Additionally, it aids in shielding the skin from harm caused by UV radiation and environmental toxins.
4. **Reduces the risk of eye diseases:** Vitamin C may reduce the risk of developing age-related macular degeneration (AMD) and cataracts, common eye diseases that can lead to vision loss.
5. **Helps manage high blood pressure:** Vitamin C helps lower blood pressure in hypertensive patients.

6. **Promotes wound healing:** Vitamin C is responsible for producing collagen necessary for wound healing. It also helps prevent infections and reduce inflammation, which can speed up the healing process.
7. **Improves mood and reduces stress:** Vitamin C improves mood and lowers stress levels by reducing cortisol levels, a stress hormone, in the body.
8. **Enhances iron absorption:** Vitamin C can enhance the absorption of Iron from plant-based foods, which is vital for vegetarians and vegans who may have lower iron levels.

ROLE OF VITAMIN C IN BRAIN HEALTH

Vitamin C, also known as ascorbic acid, plays an essential role in brain health. It is a water-soluble vitamin involved in several physiological functions within the brain, including the production of neurotransmitters, antioxidant protection, and modulation of inflammation. Here are some ways in which vitamin C contributes to brain health:

1. **Production of neurotransmitters:** Vitamin C is involved in the synthesis of several neurotransmitters, such as dopamine, norepinephrine, and serotonin. These neurotransmitters are essential for regulating mood, motivation, and cognitive function.
2. **Antioxidant protection:** The antioxidant properties of vitamin C are instrumental in safeguarding the brain against the harm caused by oxidative stress. Oxidative stress arises when there's an inequity between the formation of free radicals and the body's ability to counteract them. This can result in cellular damage and inflammation, which links to neurodegenerative illnesses like Alzheimer's and Parkinson's.
3. **Modulation of inflammation:** Vitamin C modulates inflammation in the brain by reducing the production of pro-inflammatory cytokines. Chronic inflammation in the

brain is a common feature of neurodegenerative diseases. It can contribute to the loss of neurons and cognitive decline.

4. **Neuroprotection:** Vitamin C may have neuroprotective effects by promoting the survival and growth of neurons in the brain. It may also help prevent or delay the onset of neurodegenerative diseases by reducing oxidative stress, inflammation, and cell death.
5. **Enhancing cognitive function:** Vitamin C improves cognitive function in healthy individuals and those with cognitive impairment. It may improve attention, memory, and executive function by enhancing neurotransmitter production and reducing oxidative stress.
6. **Improving mood:** Vitamin C also improves mood by reducing cortisol levels, a stress hormone that can contribute to anxiety and depression.

FOOD SOURCES OF VITAMIN C AND WAYS TO CONSUME IT

Vitamin C is present in various foods, especially fruits and vegetables. Here are some excellent food sources of vitamin C:

1. **Citrus fruits:** Oranges, lemons, limes, grapefruits, and tangerines are all rich in vitamin C.
2. **Berries:** Strawberries, raspberries, blackberries, and blueberries are excellent sources of vitamin C.
3. **Kiwifruit:** This fruit is high in vitamin C and is also a good source of fibre.
4. **Melons:** Cantaloupe and honeydew melons are high in vitamin C.
5. **Papaya:** This tropical fruit is a great source of vitamin C and also contains enzymes that aid digestion.
6. **Pineapple:** Pineapple is rich in vitamin C and also contains bromelain, an enzyme that has anti-inflammatory properties.

7. **Tomatoes:** Tomatoes are a good source of vitamin C and also contain the antioxidant lycopene.
8. **Leafy greens:** Kale, fenugreek, spinach, and other leafy greens are rich in vitamin C and other nutrients.

RECOMMENDED DIETARY ALLOWANCE

The recommended daily intake for adults is 75-90 mg daily for both women and men. However, some individuals may require higher amounts, such as smokers or those with certain medical conditions. In such cases, vitamin C supplements may be necessary.

References

1. https://ods.od.nih.gov/factsheets/VitaminC-HealthProfessional/
2. https://medlineplus.gov/ency/article/000355.htm
3. https://www.cdc.gov/nutrition/micronutrient-malnutrition/micronutrients/health-effects/scurvy.html

Zinc

WHAT IS ZINC?

Zinc is among the essential minerals in the body after Iron. It is a crucial mineral that is neither stored nor produced in the body. And thus, it needs to be outsourced through food or supplements. Zinc is vital for numerous bodily functions, including enzymatic activity, immunity, gene expression, DNA and protein synthesis, wound healing, and growth and development.

It is an essential mineral for pregnant women, lactating mothers, children and infants. The total amount of Zinc in women is 1.5 mg; in men, it is 2.5 mg, and skeletal muscles store most of it.

HEALTH BENEFITS OF ZINC

Zinc has abundant health benefits. It has proven to be effective even during the deadliest viral and bacterial attacks on humans, owing to its role in maintaining the immunity of the body.

Discussed below are other health benefits of Zinc

- **Boosts the immune system:** Zinc helps keep the immune system healthy and ready to combat any infection in the body. It functions in the enzymatic activities associated with cell function and signalling. Its deficiency often leads to a weakened immune response.
- **Acceleration of wound healing:** Hospitals commonly use Zinc for treating ulcers, burns, and skin injuries. This mineral promotes collagen synthesis and improves immune function and inflammatory response in the body. Therefore, it enhances recovery.
- **Risk reduction of certain age-related diseases:** It is a well-known fact that Zinc lowers your chances of having age-related disorders such as infections, pneumonia, AMD or age-related macular degeneration, and other cognitive and behavioural health issues. In addition, Zinc relieves oxidative stress and improves the body's natural defence mechanism. It enhances the activity of T-cells and the natural killer cells, the main immune response cells of the body.
- **Treats Acne and Lowers Inflammation:** Acne is a common issue faced by so many people. It is more common in females than in males. It is estimated to affect over 9.4% of the world's population. Acne occurs due to obstruction of the oil-producing glands in the skin by dirt, pollution, dead skin, etc. As a result, bacterial infection and inflammation occur.

Studies suggest that Zinc is good for treating acne, be it with an oral supplement or topical application. It acts by reducing inflammation and inhibiting the growth of the responsible bacteria. Furthermore, it suppresses the oil gland activity in the skin. People who are commonly affected by acne often have lower levels of Zinc.

ROLE OF ZINC IN BRAIN HEALTH

As already established, Zinc is a trace mineral that supports brain function. It is responsible for maintaining the hormones responsible for maintaining emotions, such as dopamine and serotonin. It is closely related to sustaining dopamine, a hormone responsible for memory and focus. Zinc supplements have proven to be effective in improving memory and cognitive function and have reduced impulsivity in patients with ADHD.

FOOD SOURCES AND HOW TO CONSUME THEM

Various food sources and supplements provide Zinc, which is an essential mineral. Animal proteins, such as beef, lamb, and pork, are known to be the best sources of Zinc. The dark meat of chicken also has more amounts of Zinc than fish and light meat. For vegetarians, a good source of Zinc would be whole grains, legumes, nuts and yeast.

Some of the most popular sources of Zinc include:

- **Shellfish:** oysters, crab, mussels, lobster, and clams
- **Meat:** beef, pork, lamb, and bison
- **Poultry:** turkey and chicken
- **Nuts and seeds** such as pumpkin seeds, cashews, hemp seeds
- **Dairy products:** milk, yoghourt, and cheese
- **Eggs**
- **Whole grains:** oats, quinoa, brown rice, etc.
- **Fish:** flounder, sardines, salmon, and sole

- **Legumes:** chickpeas, lentils, black beans, kidney beans
- **Certain vegetables:** mushrooms, asparagus, kale, peas, and beet greens

Even though Zinc is beneficial, there's a limit to its intake. The recommended dietary allowance of Zinc is:

- **Infants:** 2 mg/day
- **Children and infants:** between 3 to 5 mg/day
- **Teenagers:** 8 mg/day
- **Adolescents and Adults**
- **Males:** 11 mg/day
- **Females:** 8-10 mg/day

The RDA for pregnant and lactating women increases to around 10-12 mg/day.

References

1. https://medlineplus.gov/ency/article/002416.htm
2. https://www.healthline.com/nutrition/zinc
3. https://www.hsph.harvard.edu/nutritionsource/zinc/
4. https://pubmed.ncbi.nlm.nih.gov/7082716/
5. https://www.mdriveformen.com/blogs/the-driven/what-are-the-benefits-of-zinc-for-brain-health

Choline

WHAT IS CHOLINE?

Choline is a vital nutrient which our body requires for various functions. Often grouped with B vitamins, it is a water-soluble compound.

Choline plays an important role in several bodily functions, including cell membrane structure and function, nerve signalling, metabolism, and liver function. Moreover, it is involved in the synthesis of the neurotransmitter acetylcholine, which is essential for memory and cognitive function.

Choline is present in various foods, such as eggs, liver, meat, fish, nuts, and vegetables. The body can also produce it in small amounts, but most people need to obtain it from their diet to meet their daily needs.

HEALTH BENEFITS OF CHOLINE

Choline has several health benefits, including supporting brain health, liver function, and cardiovascular health.

1. **Liver function:** Choline is crucial in maintaining liver function and guarding against liver damage.
2. **Cardiovascular health:** Choline contributes to cardiovascular well-being by lowering inflammation and promoting proper blood vessel function.
3. **Athletic performance:** Choline improves athletic performance by reducing fatigue and improving muscle endurance.
4. **Pregnancy and breastfeeding:** Choline is particularly important for pregnant and breastfeeding women. It is required for foetal brain development and can help prevent neural tube defects.

ROLE OF CHOLINE IN BRAIN HEALTH

Choline plays a vital role in maintaining brain health and cognitive function. It is an essential nutrient required for the production of acetylcholine. This neurotransmitter regulates our memory, mood and attention.

Choline also helps with the formation and maintenance of the cell membranes in the brain, which are essential for the proper functioning of neurons. It also aids in the production of myelin, a substance that covers nerve fibres and facilitates nerve signalling.

Researches have shown that higher choline intake is associated with improved cognitive performance and a reduced risk of cognitive decline and dementia. A study conducted on elderly people found that higher dietary choline intake was associated with improved cognitive performance and a decreased risk of dementia.

Doctors believe that Choline plays a role in foetal brain development, and doctors advise pregnant women to consume adequate amounts of Choline to ensure proper brain development of their foetus.

FOOD SOURCES AND HOW TO CONSUME IT/RDA

There are various food sources to obtain Choline, including:

- **Eggs:** One large egg contains about 147 milligrams (mg) of Choline.
- **Meat:** Beef liver, chicken liver, and turkey contain high amounts of Choline.
- **Seafood:** Salmon, cod, shrimp, and scallops are rich in Choline. For example, 100 grams of salmon contains about 70 mg of Choline, while 100 grams of shrimp contains about 126 mg of Choline.
- **Dairy:** Milk, cheese, and yoghurt contain moderate amounts of Choline. For example, one cup of milk contains about 43 mg of Choline, while one ounce of cheddar cheese contains about 12 mg of Choline.
- **Vegetables:** Broccoli, Brussels sprouts, and cauliflower are good plant-based sources of Choline.

The recommended dietary allowance (RDA) for Choline varies by age and gender:

- **Infants:** 125-150 mg
- **Children:** 200-550 mg
- **Adolescents:** 550-850 mg
- **Adults:** 425-550 mg for women and 550 mg for men
- **Pregnant women:** 450-550 mg
- **Breastfeeding women:** 550 mg

References

1. https://ods.od.nih.gov/factsheets/Choline-HealthProfessional/#:~:text=Choline%20is%20an%20essential%20nutrient,phospholipids%20vital%20for%20cell%20membranes.
2. https://my.clevelandclinic.org/health/drugs/22202-choline-supplement
3. https://www.healthline.com/nutrition/what-is-choline#bottom-line
4. https://www.medicalnewstoday.com/articles/327117
5. https://www.webmd.com/vitamins/ai/ingredientmono-436/choline
6. https://www.ncbi.nlm.nih.gov/pmc/articles/PMC4591635/

Mono-saturated fatty acids

WHAT ARE MONO-SATURATED FATTY ACIDS?

Monounsaturated fatty acids (MUFA) are a type of unsaturated fat that contain only one double bond in their chemical structure. Unlike saturated fats, which can increase the risk of heart disease and other health problems, monounsaturated fats are heart-healthy fats. They are a healthy form of fat that provides numerous health benefits when taken in moderation.

HEALTH BENEFITS OF MONO-SATURATED FATTY ACIDS

Monounsaturated fatty acids (MUFAs) provide a variety of health benefits, which include:

1. **Improved heart health:** Studies have shown that diets high in MUFAs can help lower LDL or bad cholesterol levels and lower the risk of heart disease and stroke.
2. **Reduced inflammation:** MUFAs have anti-inflammatory properties, which can help reduce inflammation in the body.
3. **Improved insulin sensitivity:** MUFAs improve insulin sensitivity.
4. **Weight management:** MUFAs can help with weight management by making you feel full and reducing cravings for unhealthy foods. They can also boost metabolism and increase the amount of calories burned at rest, making it easier to maintain a healthy weight.
5. **Brain health:** MUFAs are important for brain health and cognitive function. They can help improve memory, mood, and overall brain function. They may also reduce the risk of age-related cognitive decline.
6. **Reduced cancer risk:** MUFAs lower the risk of certain kinds of cancer, such as breast cancer and prostate cancer.
7. **Improved fertility:** MUFAs can improve fertility in both men and women. They can help regulate hormones and improve overall reproductive function.
8. **Skin health:** MUFAs can help improve skin health by reducing inflammation and supporting healthy skin cell function.

ROLE OF MONO-SATURATED FATTY ACIDS IN BRAIN HEALTH

Mono-saturated fatty acids (MUFAs) play an important role in brain health and cognitive function. The brain contains 60% fat, and MUFAs are one of the types of fats essential for brain health. Some ways in which MUFAs can support brain health include:

1. **Improves memory and cognitive function:** MUFAs can help improve memory and cognitive function by supporting the formation and maintenance of healthy brain cell membranes. They can also help reduce inflammation in the brain, improving overall brain function.
2. **Reduces the risk of cognitive decline:** MUFAs help lower the chances of age-related cognitive decline and dementia. Studies have shown that diets rich in MUFAs can help preserve cognitive function and reduce the risk of cognitive decline.
3. **Improves mood and mental health:** MUFAs may help improve mood and mental health by reducing inflammation and supporting healthy brain cell function. They can also help regulate hormones and neurotransmitters that are important for mood and mental health.
4. **Reduces the risk of neurological disorders:** MUFAs may help reduce the risk of neurological disorders such as Parkinson's disease and Alzheimer's disease. They can help protect brain cells from damage and improve overall brain function.
5. **Improved brain development:** MUFAs are important for brain development in infants and children. They can help support healthy brain cell formation and improve cognitive function.

FOOD SOURCES AND HOW TO CONSUME IT/RDA

Mono unsaturated fatty acids (MUFAs) are present in a variety of foods, including plant-based sources and some animal products. Some of the best food sources for MUFAs include:

1. **Olive oil:** It is one of the richest sources of MUFAs. It is commonly used in Mediterranean diets and can be used for cooking or as a salad dressing.
2. **Avocado:** Avocado is another excellent source of MUFAs. You can make guacamole or salad using it.
3. **Nuts and seeds:** Nuts and seeds, like cashews, almonds, peanuts, and sesame seeds, are rich in MUFAs. They are often taken as a snack or added to salads, oatmeal, or smoothies.
4. **Peanut butter:** This is a good source of MUFAs and can be used as a spread or added to smoothies.

The recommended daily intake of MUFAs varies depending on age, sex, and physical activity level. However, the American Heart Association recommends that MUFAs should make up around 20-25% of daily calorie intake. This equates to about 13-18 grams per day for a 2000-calorie diet. It is important to consume MUFAs as part of a balanced diet. This diet should include a variety of other healthy foods, too.

References

1. https://www.ncbi.nlm.nih.gov/books/NBK92775/
2. https://www.healthline.com/nutrition/17-health-benefits-of-omega-3
3. https://fdc.nal.usda.gov/
4. https://www.heart.org/en/healthy-living/healthy-eating/eat-smart/fats/monounsaturated-fats

Carvacrol

Carvacrol is a natural compound found in the essential oils of various herbs and plants, including oregano, thyme, and savoury. It is known for its unique aroma and flavour. It has been used for centuries in traditional medicine to treat various ailments. In recent years, carvacrol has gained increasing attention for its potential health benefits, including its ability to improve brain health.

HEALTH BENEFITS OF CARVACROL

1. **Anti-inflammatory Properties:** The anti-inflammatory properties of carvacrol are potent, and they can aid in diminishing inflammation throughout the body.
2. **Antioxidant Properties:** Carvacrol is also known for its potent antioxidant properties, which can aid in shielding the body from oxidative stress.
3. **Antimicrobial Properties:** Carvacrol has potent antimicrobial properties, which can help protect against bacterial and fungal infections.
4. **Benefits to Brain Health:** Research has demonstrated that carvacrol possesses neuroprotective properties, capable of safeguarding the brain from damage and enhancing cognitive performance.

ROLE OF CARVACROL IN BRAIN HEALTH

Carvacrol has neuroprotective properties, which means it can protect the brain against damage and improve cognitive function. Studies have found that carvacrol can help improve memory and learning, protect against oxidative stress, and reduce inflammation in the brain.

Inflammation in the brain is also a common underlying factor in many neurodegenerative diseases. Carvacrol has potential anti-inflammatory properties. Thus, they can protect against the development of brain-related diseases.

Several studies have investigated the effects of carvacrol on cognitive function in animals. One study published in the Journal of Neurochemistry found that carvacrol improved cognitive function and protected against oxidative stress in rats. The researchers concluded that carvacrol might have the potential as a therapeutic agent for treating neurodegenerative diseases.

Another study investigated the effects of carvacrol on memory and learning in mice. The study found that carvacrol improved memory and learning in the mice, and the researchers suggested that carvacrol could be a promising candidate for the development of new drugs for treating cognitive impairment.

Carvacrol also has a positive effect on mood and anxiety. A study published in the journal Phytotherapy Research found that carvacrol reduced anxiety-like behaviour in mice, and the researchers suggested that carvacrol may be helpful as an anxiolytic agent.

FOOD SOURCES OF CARVACROL

1. **Oregano:** Oregano is one of the richest sources of carvacrol. It is common in Mediterranean cuisine. However, one can also add them to stews, sauces, soups, and marinades.
2. **Thyme:** Thyme is another herb that is high in carvacrol. Mediterranean and Middle Eastern cuisine often use it in soups, stews, and roasted vegetables.
3. **Savoury:** Savory is a herb that is native to the Mediterranean region and has a slightly bitter taste.
4. **Essential Oils:** Essential oils extracted from oregano, thyme, and savoury are also rich sources of carvacrol. Aromatherapy and diffusers use these oils to improve cognitive function and reduce inflammation.

RDA

Currently, there is no established Recommended Dietary Allowance (RDA) for carvacrol as it is not considered an essential nutrient.

References

1. https://www.sciencedirect.com/topics/chemistry/carvacrol
2. https://greenfieldbotanics.com/blogs/oregano-oil-and-organic-skincare/this-is-how-oregano-oil-can-improve-your-mental-health
3. https://www.ncbi.nlm.nih.gov/pmc/articles/PMC9516402/

Curcumin

Curcumin is a phytonutrient found in turmeric, a household spice in India. It is often an ingredient in yellow mustard as well. Turmeric is a very popular Ayurvedic medicine, used for thousands of years as an antiseptic and anti-inflammatory agent. It also helps reduce pain and heals wounds faster than they normally would.

As research progressed, they studied its effectiveness in improving brain health also. Recent trials suggest that curcumin may be beneficial for managing depression, anxiety, and other mental health conditions such as schizophrenia. It also suggests that curcumin is structurally a polyphenol widely found in nature. Apart from Curcumin, many other flavonoid-rich herbs, such as grape seed, pine bark, and green tea, are being researched for their potential brain health benefits.

HEALTH BENEFITS OF CURCUMIN

Curcumin is a natural compound found in turmeric. There are extensive studies on its potential health benefits, and here are some of the most promising benefits:

1. **Anti-inflammatory properties:** Studies have indicated that curcumin has substantial anti-inflammatory effects, which may be beneficial in mitigating symptoms associated with inflammatory disorders like rheumatoid arthritis, osteoarthritis, and inflammatory bowel disease.
2. **Antioxidant properties:** Curcumin is a potent antioxidant that can aid in shielding cells from damage inflicted by free radicals. Consequently, it may reduce the likelihood of chronic illnesses such as cancer, Alzheimer's disease, and heart disease.
3. **Pain relief:** Studies have demonstrated that curcumin exhibits analgesic properties and may be especially helpful in reducing joint pain and stiffness in individuals with arthritis.
4. **Reduced risk of heart disease:** Curcumin may help lower the risk of heart disease by improving blood vessel function, reducing inflammation, and lowering cholesterol levels.
5. **Improved digestion:** Curcumin has a potential benefits for digestion by alleviating symptoms associated with digestive disorders such as IBS.
6. **Potential anticancer properties:** Curcumin has anticancer properties, as shown in some studies, and it may help reduce the risk of certain types of cancer, such as colorectal cancer.

ROLE OF CURCUMIN IN BRAIN HEALTH

Studies show the potential role of Curcumin in brain health. Curcumin may be beneficial for the brain in the following ways:

1. **Cognitive enhancement:** Curcumin has cognitive-enhancing effects, which can help improve memory and attention span. Additionally, some studies have found that Curcumin may improve mood and reduce symptoms of depression.

2. **Neuroprotective effects:** Curcumin has neuroprotective effects, which can help protect against neurodegenerative diseases such as Alzheimer's and Parkinson's diseases. Curcumin may help prevent the accumulation of beta-amyloid plaques in the brain, which are a hallmark of Alzheimer's disease.
3. **Neuroplasticity enhancement:** Curcumin can enhance neuroplasticity, which refers to the brain's ability to change and adapt in response to new experiences. Improved neuroplasticity can help improve learning and memory.
4. **Increased BDNF:** Curcumin increases brain-derived neurotrophic factor (BDNF) levels, which can promote brain health and protect against neurodegenerative diseases.

FOOD SOURCES OF CURCUMIN AND HOW TO CONSUME IT.

Curcumin is naturally present in turmeric. However, the amount of curcumin in turmeric is relatively low, so it may be challenging to consume enough curcumin through diet alone. Here are some food sources of curcumin:

1. **Turmeric:** As mentioned, turmeric is the primary dietary source of curcumin. Turmeric is used in cooking to add flavour and colour to a variety of dishes.
2. **Curry powder:** This powder is a blend of spices that often includes turmeric, so it can be a good source of curcumin.
3. **Mustard:** Mustard seeds and the condiment made from them contain curcumin.
4. **Ginger:** Ginger is another spice that contains curcumin, although in smaller amounts than turmeric.
5. **Supplements:** Curcumin supplements are also available in the market in the form of capsules or tablets and can provide a concentrated dose of curcumin.

RECOMMENDED DIETARY ALLOWANCE

There is no established Recommended Dietary Allowance (RDA) for curcumin, as it is not considered an essential nutrient. However, the World Health Organization (WHO) has established an Acceptable Daily Intake (ADI) of Curcumin at 0-3 mg per kg of body weight per day based on safety considerations.

References

1. https://www.ncbi.nlm.nih.gov/pmc/articles/PMC5664031/
2. https://www.liebertpub.com/doi/10.1089/jmf.2016.3705
3. https://www.ncbi.nlm.nih.gov/pmc/articles/PMC7728608/
4. https://www.everydayhealth.com/depression/whats-the-deal-with-turmeric-for-depression/
5. https://pubmed.ncbi.nlm.nih.gov/31423805/
6. https://pubmed.ncbi.nlm.nih.gov/31423805/
7. https://www.healthline.com/health/depression/turmeric-for-depression

Ferulic acid

WHAT IS FERULIC ACID?

Ferulic acid is a type of organic compound that belongs to the class of hydroxycinnamic acids. Ferulic acid is known for its antioxidant properties, often used in skincare products, food preservation, and dietary supplements and found commonly in various plant sources, such as rice bran, wheat, oats, and coffee.

HEALTH BENEFITS OF FERULIC ACID

You may find that ferulic acid has various potential benefits for your health. It possesses antioxidant, anti-inflammatory, and antimicrobial properties. Skincare products reduce or even reverse the signs of ageing, protect the skin from sun damage, and prevent skin cancer.

ANTI-AGEING EFFECTS

Ferulic acid is famous for its potential anti-ageing properties, primarily due to its antioxidant effects that combat free radicals, which contribute to skin ageing, such as wrinkles and age spots.

It may protect vital structures like collagen and elastin and also enhance the effectiveness of other common antioxidants like vitamins A, C, and E.

Ferulic acid also reduces the production of melanin, the skin pigment, which could lighten age spots.

PROTECTION FROM SUN DAMAGE

When used with vitamins C and E, ferulic acid provides protective benefits against sun damage. Its antioxidant activity is said to guard the skin against the harmful effects of UV radiation, which are associated with skin cancer development. However, to receive this benefit, apply ferulic acid before exposure to the sun. This is because it cannot reverse the damage that has already occurred but only prevent it from occurring again.

ROLE OF FERULIC ACID IN BRAIN HEALTH

Researches show that as people become old, their brains are more likely to experience oxidative stress, which can lead to neurodegenerative diseases like Alzheimer's.

This happens when free radicals damage important parts of cells, like proteins and DNA. Ferulic acid can help protect cells from free radicals by getting rid of them before they can cause damage.

FOOD SOURCES OF FERULIC ACID

If you are looking to increase your intake of ferulic acid, there are several food sources you can turn to. Whole grains like oats, brown rice and barley are good sources of ferulic acid. In addition, fruits like apples, oranges, pineapples, and grapes contain ferulic acid.

Vegetables such as tomatoes, spinach, and sweet corn are good sources of this antioxidant. Nuts such as almonds and peanuts and seeds like flax seeds and sesame seeds are also rich in ferulic acid. Adding these foods to your daily diet can increase your intake of ferulic acid.

RECOMMENDED DIETARY ALLOWANCE

There is currently no Recommended Dietary Allowance (RDA) for ferulic acid established by the National Institutes of Health (NIH). This is because ferulic acid is an essential nutrient, meaning that the body can produce it on its own or obtain it from food sources.

References

1. https://www.medicalnewstoday.com/articles/ferulic-acid
2. https://www.healthline.com/health/ferulic-acid
3. https://www.verywellhealth.com/the-benefits-of-ferulic-acid-89607
4. https://www.webmd.com/diet/foods-high-in-ferulic-acid
5. https://www.ncbi.nlm.nih.gov/pmc/articles/PMC2127228/

Theanine

WHAT IS THEANINE?

Theanine, also known as L-theanine, is an amino acid commonly found in tea leaves, particularly green tea. It is known for its calming effects and acts as a natural remedy for anxiety, stress, and insomnia.

Theanine works by increasing levels of GABA (gamma-aminobutyric acid), a neurotransmitter in the brain that helps regulate mood and promote relaxation. It also helps increase alpha waves in the brain, which are associated with relaxation and alertness.

HEALTH BENEFITS OF THEANINE

Theanine is a crucial phytonutrient which improves health significantly. Let us discuss the various health benefits it offers with respect to different body systems.

1. Reducing stress and anxiety
2. Improving sleep quality
3. Boosting cognitive function
4. Supporting cardiovascular health
5. Reducing inflammation

ROLE OF THEANINE IN BRAIN HEALTH

While Theanine is not a replacement for prescribed medication for depression, some evidences suggest that it may help alleviate symptoms of depression in some individuals. Here are some ways in which Theanine may help improve depression symptoms:

1. **Boosting mood:** Theanine has been shown to have a calming effect on the brain, which can improve mood and alleviate feelings of stress and anxiety. By increasing levels of GABA, a neurotransmitter that helps regulate mood and promote relaxation, Theanine may help alleviate symptoms of depression.
2. **Reducing inflammation:** Some studies have suggested that Theanine may have anti-inflammatory effects, which could benefit individuals with depression.
3. **Improving sleep:** Theanine has been shown to help enhance the quality of sleep, which can be especially important for individuals with depression.

4. **Enhancing cognitive function:** Theanine improves cognitive function, including attention, focus, and memory.
5. **Potentially reducing medication side effects:** While there is a need for more research in this area, some studies have suggested that Theanine may help reduce some side effects associated with antidepressant medications.

FOOD SOURCES OF THEANINE

Suppose you're looking to increase your intake of Theanine. In that case, there are several food sources that you can incorporate into your diet. First, let us discuss some important sources of Theanine:

1. Green tea
2. Black tea
3. White tea
4. Mushrooms
5. Algae

A few cups a day can provide a significant amount of Theanine, whether you prefer green tea, black tea, or white tea. Additionally, incorporating mushrooms and algae into your diet can also help boost your intake of this beneficial amino acid.

RECOMMENDED DIETARY ALLOWANCE

The Recommended Dietary Allowance (RDA) of Theanine has yet to be established, as it is not considered an essential nutrient. Theanine is a non-essential amino acid, meaning that the body can synthesize it on its own and does not require dietary intake to function properly.

References

1. https://pubmed.ncbi.nlm.nih.gov/18296328/
2. https://www.healthline.com/health/l-theanine

3. https://www.webmd.com/vitamins/ai/ingredientmono-1053/theanine

Proanthocyanidins

The grape seed extract is a byproduct of grape seeds used commonly in the industry. It is packed with antioxidants and oligomeric proanthocyanidin complexes and is associated with various potential health benefits, including the treatment of ailments like hyperlipidemia, atherosclerosis, macular degeneration, poor circulation, and nerve damage.

Although many of these health claims lack substantial evidence, some studies have supported their use. Consumption of grape seed extract can be in the form of a liquid, tablets, or capsules, and dietary supplements usually contain 50 to 100 milligrams of the extract.

BENEFITS

Animal studies have demonstrated the potential of grape seed extract in treating heart disease, and some experts speculate that it may also possess anticancer and chemopreventive properties. There has been significant research in recent years investigating the therapeutic properties of grape seed extract, with several important discoveries made. Some of the main findings are given below.

Healing wounds

Grape seed extract has the potential to accelerate wound healing, as per a popular study. In the study, proanthocyanidin extract derived from grape seeds was applied topically to wounds on the backs of mice, resulting in faster healing times.

Improving bone strength

A study suggests that consuming grape seed extract along with calcium may positively impact bone strength and formation, particularly in cases where low levels of calcium cause bone debility.

Anti-Candida activity

An Italian study investigated the potential of grape seed extract to combat Candida, a parasitic fungus that can cause thrush. The extract, which contains flavan-3-ols, was found to inhibit the growth of Candida albicans after five days of exposure.

The researchers concluded that grape seed extracts with a high concentration of polymeric flavan-3-ols aid in the treatment of mucosal infections such as vaginal candidiasis.

Preventing skin cancer

Proanthocyanidins found in grape seeds may have cancer-preventing properties. The protective properties of proanthocyanidins may be due to several factors, including reducing oxidative stress and altering cytokine activity to suppress the immune system.

Cardiovascular benefits

The antioxidants present in grape seed extract have the potential to protect blood vessels from damage, thereby reducing the risk of developing high blood pressure. A study found that grape seed proanthocyanidin extract (GSPE) had better antioxidant efficacy than Vitamins C, E, and β-carotene.

Other possible benefits

The grape seed extract has potential benefits in treating tooth decay, protecting against pathogens, improving night vision, treating diabetic retinopathy, improving blood sugar control, and reducing oedema. It may also have anti-ageing properties by protecting collagen and elastin, reducing inflammation, and reducing iron levels in people with hemochromatosis.

ROLE OF PROANTHOCYANIDINS IN BRAIN HEALTH

Proanthocyanidins have a number of potential benefits for brain health, such as:

- **Antioxidant effects:** Proanthocyanidins are potent antioxidants, which means that they can help to protect the brain from oxidative stress. It also protects the brain from free radicals. As a result, the chances of cognitive decline and other age-related neurological disorders are lower.
- **Anti-inflammatory effects:** Inflammation plays a role in many neurological disorders, including Alzheimer's disease and depression. Proanthocyanidins have anti-inflammatory effects.
- **Neuroprotective effects:** Proanthocyanidins have neuroprotective effects, which means that they can help protect brain cells from damage and death.
- **Mood-enhancing effects:** Some studies have suggested that proanthocyanidins may have mood-enhancing effects and may help reduce symptoms of depression and anxiety. This may be due in part to their ability to increase the levels of certain neurotransmitters in the brain, including dopamine and serotonin, which are important for regulating mood and emotional well-being.
- **Cognitive-enhancing effects:** Proanthocyanidins have cognitive-enhancing effects, which means that they help improve cognitive functions, such as attention, memory, and executive function.

FOOD SOURCES OF PROANTHOCYANIDINS

Proanthocyanidins are present in a variety of plant-based foods, such as:

- Berries
- Grapes
- Cocoa and chocolate
- Nuts
- Red wine

- Tea
- Apples
- Pomegranates

RECOMMENDED DIETARY ALLOWANCE

There is currently no established Recommended Dietary Allowance (RDA) or Daily Value (DV) for proanthocyanidins. Since these compounds are not essential nutrients, there is no established daily intake level that is necessary to maintain health.

References

1. https://www.medicalnewstoday.com/articles/271156
2. https://www.tandfonline.com/doi/abs/10.1080/01478885.2020.1861907
3. https://www.nutraceuticalbusinessreview.com/news/article_page/Flavonoid_intake_associated_with_decreased_depression_risk/132958

Quercetin

WHAT IS QUERCETIN?

Quercetin is a nutrient or a naturally occurring flavonoid found in a variety of plant-based foods, including fruits, vegetables, and grains. It belongs to the class of compounds known as polyphenols, known for their potent antioxidant and anti-inflammatory properties.

In addition to its antioxidant and anti-inflammatory effects, Quercetin has a number of other potential health benefits. For example, it may help lower blood pressure and help regulate blood sugar levels in people with diabetes. In addition, it improves exercise performance and reduces symptoms of respiratory infections.

While Quercetin is generally safe when consumed in food, the safety of high-dose supplements is not well evident. Some studies have suggested that high doses may cause side effects, including headaches, stomach upset, and kidney damage.

ROLE OF QUERCETIN IN BRAIN HEALTH

Quercetin has been studied for its potential role in brain health, particularly its antioxidant and anti-inflammatory effects, which may protect against oxidative stress and inflammation, both of which may affect the pathogenesis of neurodegenerative diseases. Some examples include Alzheimer's and Parkinson's disease.

Quercetin has potential benefits in the prevention and treatment of other neurological disorders, such as depression and anxiety.

HEALTH BENEFITS OF QUERCETIN

1. Quercetin is a potent antioxidant that helps protect your body from free radical damage, which can lead to chronic diseases such as cancer and cardiovascular disease.
2. It has anti-inflammatory properties that may help reduce inflammation in your body, which is associated with many health problems, including arthritis, asthma, and autoimmune disorders.
3. Quercetin may help improve cardiovascular health.
4. It may also help improve your immune function.
5. Quercetin has potential benefits for brain health, including improving cognitive function, memory, and learning and protecting against neurodegenerative diseases such as Alzheimer's and Parkinson's.

6. It may also have anticancer properties, as studies have found that Quercetin can help inhibit the growth and spread of cancer cells.
7. Quercetin may improve exercise performance by increasing endurance and reducing fatigue.
8. It has anti-allergy properties, which may help to reduce symptoms of allergies and asthma.
9. Quercetin may also help protect your skin from damage caused by UV radiation, which can lead to premature ageing and skin cancer.

FOOD SOURCES AND HOW TO CONSUME IT

1. **Fruits:** Some of the best fruit sources of Quercetin include apples, berries, cherries, grapes, and citrus fruits.
2. **Vegetables:** Many vegetables, including onions, broccoli, spinach, kale, and tomatoes, are also good sources of Quercetin. To consume Quercetin from vegetables, try incorporating them into your meals in a variety of ways, such as adding onions to your soups and stews, making a spinach salad, or roasting broccoli as a side dish.
3. **Herbs and spices:** Quercetin is also present in a variety of herbs and spices, including parsley, cilantro, capers, and dill. To consume Quercetin from herbs and spices, use them as seasonings for your meals, such as adding fresh herbs to your salads or using capers to flavour your sauces.

RECOMMENDED DIETARY ALLOWANCE

Although there is no established Recommended Dietary Allowance (RDA) for Quercetin, it is generally safe to consume in moderate amounts as part of a healthy and balanced diet.

REFERENCES

1. https://pubmed.ncbi.nlm.nih.gov/27651256/
2. https://www.ncbi.nlm.nih.gov/pmc/articles/PMC9027262/

3. https://www.healthline.com/nutrition/quercetin
4. https://www.health.com/quercetin-health-benefits-6825553

Resveratrol

WHAT IS RESVERATROL?

Resveratrol is a natural substance that belongs to the polyphenol family and is present in the skin of red grapes, peanuts, and certain berries. It promotes its potential health benefits and is known to have antioxidant properties.

Resveratrol gained popularity after several studies suggested that it could have anti-ageing, anti-inflammatory, and anti-cancer effects. It also has potential benefits for heart health, brain function, and diabetes.

HEALTH AND BRAIN BENEFITS OF RESVERATROL

Resveratrol is a naturally occurring substance in several plants, including grapes, peanuts, and berries. Some researches suggest that it may have several potential health and brain benefits, such as:

1. **Anti-inflammatory effects:** Resveratrol has anti-inflammatory effects, which may benefit brain health. Chronic inflammation is associated with a range of neurological disorders, including Alzheimer's disease and Parkinson's disease.
2. **Antioxidant activity:** Resveratrol has strong antioxidant properties. This protects the brain cells from damage caused by free radicals.
3. **Neuroprotective effects:** Resveratrol has potential neuroprotective effects. This lowers the risk of age-related cognitive decline and neurodegenerative diseases.
4. **Improves cognitive function:** Some studies suggest that Resveratrol may improve cognitive function, including memory, attention, and executive function.

5. **Reduces the risk of neurodegenerative diseases:** Resveratrol has potential benefits for reducing the risk of neurodegenerative diseases.

FOOD SOURCES OF RESVERATROL

Resveratrol is present in a variety of food sources, including:

1. **Grapes:** Resveratrol is found in the skin of red and purple grapes and is a major component of red wine.
2. **Berries:** Blueberries, cranberries, and bilberries are good sources of Resveratrol.
3. **Peanuts:** Resveratrol can be present in peanuts and peanut butter.
4. **Dark chocolate:** Some types of dark chocolate contain Resveratrol.
5. **Red wine:** Red wine is a source of Resveratrol, but its consumption should be in moderation due to its alcohol content.
6. **Japanese knotweed:** This plant is a significant source of Resveratrol, but its consumption is not common as a food.

RECOMMENDED DIETARY ALLOWANCE

There is currently no Recommended Dietary Allowance (RDA) for Resveratrol, as it is not an essential nutrient. Therefore, the optimal dosage of Resveratrol for health benefits still needs to be determined. It varies depending on the condition.

References

1. https://www.frontiersin.org/articles/10.3389/fncel.2019.00030/full
2. https://www.ncbi.nlm.nih.gov/pmc/articles/PMC6225181/
3. https://www.news-medical.net/health/Can-Resveratrol-Improve-Symptoms-of-Anxiety-and-Depression.aspx

Epigallocatechin-3-gallate

WHAT IS EPIGALLOCATECHIN-3-GALLATE?

Epigallocatechin-3-gallate (EGCG) is a type of catechin, a flavonoid and a natural antioxidant found in various plants, including green tea. EGCG is the most commonly found catechin in green tea, and it has several health benefits, such as anti-inflammatory, anticancer, and neuroprotective effects. It has also been studied for its potential role in weight loss and improving heart health.

HEALTH BENEFITS OF EPIGALLOCATECHIN-3-GALLATE

Epigallocatechin-3-gallate or EGCG is a type of catechin. It is present in green tea, which has potential health benefits. Here are some of the ways EGCG may benefit your health:

1. **Anti-inflammatory effects:** While inflammation is a normal reaction to injury or infection, prolonged or chronic inflammation can lead to the onset of several conditions, such as heart disease, diabetes, and arthritis.

2. **Anti-cancer effects:** According to a literature review published in Molecules, EGCG exhibits anti-cancer properties and may be effective in inhibiting the proliferation and metastasis of certain types of cancer cells, such as breast, lung, prostate, and liver cancer cells.

3. **Neuroprotective effects:** EGCG has been shown to protect neurons from damage and may help prevent or treat neurodegenerative diseases like Alzheimer's and Parkinson's diseases.

4. **Weight loss:** EGCG has been studied for its potential to aid in weight loss and may help increase fat burning and reduce fat storage.

5. **Heart health:** EGCG improves heart health by reducing cholesterol levels, lowering blood pressure, and improving blood flow.

ROLE OF EPIGALLOCATECHIN-3-GALLATE IN BRAIN HEALTH

Some important health benefits of EGCG include:

1. **Neuroprotection:** EGCG has been shown to protect neurons from damage and may help prevent or treat neurodegenerative diseases like Alzheimer's and Parkinson's diseases.
2. **Cognitive function:** EGCG improves cognitive function, including memory and learning.
3. **Mood and anxiety:** EGCG has the potential to improve mood and reduce anxiety.
4. **Brain blood flow:** EGCG improves blood flow to the brain, which is important for brain function.
5. **Neuroinflammation:** EGCG has anti-inflammatory properties. Inflammation in the brain is associated with various neurological disorders.

FOOD SOURCES OF EPIGALLOCATECHIN-3-GALLATE

Epigallocatechin-3-gallate (EGCG) is found naturally in several food sources and is most notable in green tea. Some foods that contain EGCG are:

1. **Green tea:** Green tea is the richest source of EGCG, with an average cup containing between 50 to 150 mg of EGCG.
2. **Black tea:** Black tea also contains EGCG, although in smaller amounts than green tea.
3. **White tea:** White tea, made from the young leaves and buds of the tea plant, contains high levels of EGCG.
4. **Dark chocolate:** Dark chocolate contains small amounts of EGCG and other flavonoids.
5. **Fruits and vegetables:** Some fruits and vegetables, such as apples, strawberries, raspberries, and spinach, contain small amounts of EGCG.

RECOMMENDED DIETARY ALLOWANCE

The recommended dietary allowance (RDA) for EGCG is not official for this compound. This is because EGCG is not an essential nutrient, meaning that the body can function properly without it. However, studies suggest that consuming 200-300 mg of EGCG per day may provide health benefits.

References

1. https://pubag.nal.usda.gov/catalog/7019423
2. https://pubmed.ncbi.nlm.nih.gov/35939172/
3. https://pubmed.ncbi.nlm.nih.gov/32955535/
4. https://www.sciencedirect.com/science/article/pii/S1756464620303303
5. https://www.frontiersin.org/articles/10.3389/fnmol.2022.1109458/full
6. https://digitalcommons.pcom.edu/cgi/viewcontent.cgi?article=1201&context=pa_systematic_reviews

Berberine

WHAT IS BERBERINE?

Berberine is a natural alkaloid compound in several plants, including goldenseal, barberry, and Oregon grape. The traditional medicine of various cultures, including Ayurveda and Chinese medicine, uses it. People often use Berberine as a dye, and it has a bright yellow colour.

Berberine has numerous potential health benefits, including anti-inflammatory, antimicrobial, and antioxidant effects. In addition, it lowers blood glucose levels. It does so by increasing insulin sensitivity and reducing insulin resistance, which makes it potentially helpful in managing diabetes. Berberine also reduce cholesterol levels and improve heart health by decreasing the production of LDL cholesterol and triglycerides.

Researces have also explored the possibility that Berberine possesses properties that could combat cancer. Findings indicate that it could impede the proliferation and dissemination of cancer cells and may even enhance the efficacy of chemotherapy medications. Berberine can be acquired in supplement format and acts as a natural substitute for pharmaceutical drugs in the treatment of various ailments.

HEALTH BENEFITS OF BERBERINE

Recent studies have found that Berberine has numerous potential health benefits, including:

1. Lowering blood sugar levels
2. Improving heart health
3. Anti-inflammatory effects
4. Anti-microbial effects
5. Potential anti-cancer properties
6. Weight loss
7. Digestive Health

ROLE OF BERBERINE IN BRAIN HEALTH

One study demonstrated that Berberine was able to reduce the accumulation of beta-amyloid, a protein that links to the development of Alzheimer's disease, in the brains of mice. At the same time, another study found that Berberine was able to protect neurons from the damage caused by oxidative stress.

Berberine also has anti-inflammatory effects, which can be beneficial for brain health. Several neurological disorders, including Alzheimer's, Parkinson's, and multiple sclerosis, are associated with chronic inflammation in the brain. By reducing inflammation, Berberine may help prevent or slow the progression of these conditions.

Studies prove that Berberine also improves cognitive function and memory in animals. A study published in the journal *Behavioural Brain Research* found that Berberine improved spatial memory and learning in rats. Another study published in the Journal of Natural Medicines found that Berberine improved cognitive function in mice with Alzheimer's disease.

FOOD SOURCES OF BERBERINE

Berberine is a natural compound found in several plants, herbs, and spices. Some common food sources of Berberine include:

1. **Turmeric:** This is a spice used in Indian and Middle Eastern cuisines. It is known for its anti-inflammatory properties and is also a source of Berberine.
2. **Oregon Grape:** The Oregon grape is a shrub that is native to North America. Herbal medicine uses its roots as it contains high levels of Berberine.
3. **Chinese Skullcap:** Chinese skullcap is a herb commonly used in traditional Chinese medicine. It contains high levels of Berberine and other beneficial compounds.
4. **Coptis Chinensis:** Coptis chinensis, also known as goldthread, is a herb used in traditional Chinese medicine. It is a rich source of Berberine and has a broad range of health benefits.

RECOMMENDED DIETARY ALLOWANCE?

Berberine is available in supplement form for consumption through certain foods and herbs. The recommended daily dose of Berberine varies but generally ranges from 900 to 1500 mg per day, is divided into two or three doses. The appropriate dosage of Berberine depends on several factors, such as the reason for use, age, and overall health status.

References

1. https://www.webmd.com/vitamins/ai/ingredientmono-1126/berberine
2. https://www.healthline.com/nutrition/oregon-grape
3. https://www.nccih.nih.gov/health/turmeric

Limonoids

WHAT ARE LIMONOIDS?

Limonoids are a group of natural compounds primarily found in citrus fruits, such as oranges, lemons, and grapefruits, as well as in other plants like neem and mahogany. They are classified as a type of triterpenoid, which means they comprise three terpene units.

Limonoids have various beneficial properties, including anti-cancer, anti-inflammatory, and anti-viral activities. They are also known for promoting liver health and stimulating the immune system. Additionally, some studies have shown that limonoids may have a positive effect on cholesterol levels, blood pressure, and diabetes.

HEALTH BENEFITS OF LIMONOIDS

Limonoids are known for their health benefits and are still under research for their potential use in preventing and treating various diseases. Its health benefits are:

- Anti-cancer properties
- Immune system support
- Cholesterol-lowering properties
- Antimicrobial properties
- Liver health
- Digestive health
- Skin health
- Weight management

ROLE OF LIMONOIDS IN BRAIN HEALTH

Limonoids have a potential role in brain health. This is because of some of their properties, such as:

- **Neuroprotective properties:** Limonoids have neuroprotective properties that can help protect the brain from damage. They work by reducing oxidative stress, inflammation, and apoptosis in the brain, which are all contributing factors to neurodegenerative diseases such as Alzheimer's and Parkinson's disease.
- **Improved cognitive function:** Limonoids improve cognitive function, including memory, learning, and attention. They work by increasing the production of acetylcholine.
- **Reduced risk of Parkinson's and Alzheimer's disease:** Limonoids may also help reduce the risk of Parkinson's disease, a neurodegenerative disease. The loss of dopamine-producing neurons in the brain characterizes this disease. Limonoids protect dopamine-producing neurons from damage and reduce inflammation and oxidative stress in the brain.
- **Improved mood:** Limonoids may help improve mood by increasing the production of serotonin.
- **Protection against stroke:** Limonoids may also help protect the brain against stroke, which occurs when blood flow to the brain is interrupted. Limonoids work by reducing inflammation and oxidative stress in the brain, which are both contributing factors to stroke.

FOOD SOURCES OF LIMONOIDS

Limonoids are naturally occurring compounds that are present in citrus fruits. Here are some important food sources of limonoids:

1. **Oranges:** Orange is a rich source of limonoids, especially in the peel and pith. Eating whole fruit, including the peel, can help you obtain more limonoids.
2. **Lemons:** Lemons are another citrus fruit that is high in limonoids. The peel contains the highest concentration of limonoids, so adding lemon zest to your meals or drinking hot water with lemon juice and zest can be an excellent way to incorporate limonoids into your diet.
3. **Limes:** Limes are a great source of limonoids, particularly the peel. Adding lime zest to your dishes or using lime juice in marinades or dressings can help you obtain more limonoids.
4. **Grapefruits:** Grapefruits are another citrus fruit that contains limonoids. The peel and pith of grapefruits have the highest concentration of limonoids. Eating the fruit, including the white pith, can help you obtain more limonoids.

RECOMMENDED DIETARY ALLOWANCE

The Recommended Dietary Allowance (RDA) for limonoids is not official, as they are not considered essential nutrients. However, incorporating citrus fruits into your diet on a regular basis can provide a good amount of limonoids and support overall health, including brain health.

References

1. https://www.medicalnewstoday.com/articles/326787
2. https://www.ncbi.nlm.nih.gov/pmc/articles/PMC7468751/
3. https://resjournals.onlinelibrary.wiley.com/doi/10.1111/j.1365-3032.1990.tb00490.x

4

Regrowing Brain Cells

What is it like Living with Depression & Anxiety?

Living with anxiety and Depression can be a challenging experience. Given that it is not easy to diagnose anxiety and depression for prolonged periods, it may develop to the extent that it may start affecting your daily routine. Consequently, you may feel like you're constantly in a state of fear or worry or feeling hopeless and helpless about your life.

These feelings can affect your relationships, work or school performance, and overall quality of life. Here are some ways in which anxiety and depression can impact your life and must be identified and addressed at the earliest:

THOUGHTS AND EMOTIONS

Often, people with anxiety and depression have constant thoughts that are negative or pessimistic. For example, you may feel like you're not good enough, that everything is going wrong, or that the worst possible outcome is always going to happen. These thoughts can be overwhelming and make it difficult to focus on anything else.

RELATIONSHIPS

Prolonged and untreated anxiety and depression can put a strain on your relationships with others. You may feel like you're always on edge, which can cause you to snap at others or push them away. You may feel misunderstood and also find it challenging to connect with others.

WORK OR SCHOOL PERFORMANCE

Performance at work or school is commonly known to be reported by people having mental health issues. For example, you may have trouble in concentrating, feel overwhelmed by even simple tasks, or struggle to complete assignments or projects on time. This can lead to the feelings of guilt or shame, which can further worsen your anxiety or depression.

COPING STRATEGIES

Furthermore, you may also rely on unhealthy coping strategies to deal with your feelings. For example, you may turn to alcohol or drugs to help you relax or feel better. You may also engage in self-harm or other dangerous behaviours as a way to cope with your emotions.

CONDITIONS OF FAMILY AND FRIENDS OF THE PATIENT

One of the most common experiences for people with depression is feeling helpless. You may feel like there is nothing you can do to help your loved one or make their symptoms go away. This can be especially frustrating if you are a problem-solver and are used to making things better for your family. Remember that mental health issues are complex and require professional help and that you can still offer support and love to your loved ones even if you cannot fix everything.

Living with a loved one with anxiety and depression can also be emotionally draining. You may feel like you are constantly walking on eggshells, trying to avoid triggers or situations that could make things worse. It is essential to set boundaries for yourself and practice self-care so that you can be there for your loved ones without sacrificing your own well-being.

Communication can also be a challenge when someone is struggling with mental health issues. Your loved ones may struggle to express their emotiosns or withdraw and isolate themselves. Ensure that you keep the lines of communication open and are patient and understanding. You can try asking open-ended questions, offering non-judgmental support, and reminding your loved ones that you are there for them.

Mental health issues are not anyone's fault but occur as a result of untended emotions. In some cases, family and friends may also experience feelings of guilt or shame. You may feel like you did something to cause your loved ones' mental health issues or that you are not doing enough to help them. Timely professional help is definitely the best way to support your loved one.

HOW DO BRAIN CELLS REGROW?

To most of us, it may sound surprising that brain cells regrow. However, studies suggest that through neurogenesis, or the growth of new brain cells, some regions of the brain do regenerate throughout our lives. Let us discuss how this process of brain cell regeneration takes place and how it can benefit our overall brain health.

First, let us familiarise ourselves with the different types of cells in the brain. Typically, there are two types of cells in the brain: neurons and glial cells. Neurons are the cells that transmit information throughout the brain, while glial cells support and protect neurons. Within the brain, there are specific regions called neurogenic niches where new neurons can grow and develop.

So, how exactly do brain cells regrow? The process of neurogenesis begins with the activation of stem cells in the neurogenic niches. These stem cells, also known as neural progenitor cells, can differentiate into different types of cells in the body, including neurons and glial cells. When these cells are activated, they divide and differentiate into new neurons, which then integrate into the existing neural networks of the brain.

Various factors, including hormones, neurotransmitters, and growth factors, regulate the neurogenesis process. For example, researches shows that exercise can increase the production of a growth factor called brain-derived neurotrophic factor (BDNF), which promotes the survival and growth of new neurons in the brain. Other factors, such as stress and ageing, can negatively affect neurogenesis.

Neurogenesis primarily occurs in two regions of the brain: the hippocampus and the olfactory bulb. The hippocampus is responsible for our learning and memory, while the olfactory bulb is responsible for our sense of smell. Both of these regions continue to produce new neurons throughout our lives. However, the rate of neurogenesis decreases with age.

So, why is neurogenesis important for brain health? Studies have shown that neurogenesis plays a crucial role in many aspects of brain function, including learning, memory, and mood regulation. In animal studies, blocking neurogenesis has been shown to impair learning and memory, while increasing neurogenesis improves these cognitive functions. Additionally, some studies have suggested that neurogenesis may play a role in protecting against depression and anxiety.

While the process of brain cell regrowth may seem mysterious, it is clear that neurogenesis plays an important role in our overall brain health. As discussed above, you can promote the growth and survival of new brain cells and support optimal brain function by taking steps to support neurogenesis.

REFERENCES

1. https://www.verywellmind.com/adult-neurogenesis-can-we-grow-new-brain-cells-2794885
2. https://health.ucsd.edu/news/releases/Pages/2020-04-15-when-damaged-adult-brain-repairs-itself-going-back-to-beginning.aspx#:~:text=Instead%2C%20when%20an%20adult%20brain,an%20environment%20to%20grow%20into.

3. https://bebrainfit.com/brain-cells-regenerate/

HOW DIET HELPS MANAGE SYMPTOMS AND GROW THE NEW BRAIN CELLS

Recent studies suggest that diet is the most neglected factor in mental health issues. This is because eating a healthy and balanced diet can significantly impact your brain function and mood. Even minor modifications in the diet can manage symptoms of depression.

Several studies in the past indicated an association between the overall quality of the diet and the risk of depression. A review of 21 studies from 10 countries concluded that consumption of healthy foods, for example fruits, vegetables, pulses, whole grains, dairy, fish and animal food, etc. lowered the risk of depression.

On the other hand, a Western diet of junk food, which includes sweets, refined foods, potatoes, processed meats, red meat, and others, all lead to an increased risk of depression.

Though not significantly proven, surely there is an association between mental health and brain function with food.

In addition to providing essential nutrients, a healthy diet promotes the growth of new brain cells. This process, known as neurogenesis, is important for maintaining brain function and improving mental health. Eating a diet rich in phytonutrients and B vitamins has been shown to promote neurogenesis and improve mood.

ROLE OF THE HIPPOCAMPUS

The hippocampus is a very important part of the brain. It is involved in the functioning of memory and learning. Located in the temporal lobe of the head, it is responsible for forming and retrieving both short-term and long-term memories.

The hippocampus also plays a crucial role in spatial navigation, helping you orient yourself in your environment and remember locations.

Studies have shown that people with depression often have a smaller hippocampus compared to people who do not have depression. This suggests that the hippocampus may be affected by depression in some way.

It is involved in regulating the stress response in the body. It may not be able to perform this function when it is damaged or shrunken. This can result in an overactive stress response, a common feature of depression.

The hippocampus also plays a role in creating new memories, and as already discussed, people with depression may have difficulty in forming new memories or recalling past ones.

Furthermore, stress, dysregulation of the stress response, and impairment of mood regulation and memory formation are all potential mechanisms by which the hippocampus may contribute to depression.

References

1. https://www.ncbi.nlm.nih.gov/pmc/articles/PMC524959/#:~:text=The%20hippocampus%20is%20one%20region,central%20role%20in%20depressive%20illness
2. https://www.theguardian.com/society/2015/jun/30/chronic-depression-shrinks-brains-memories-and-emotions

Research findings indicate that individuals diagnosed with depression tend to have a smaller hippocampus, a brain structure essential for various cognitive functions, including emotional processing. The hippocampus plays a crucial role in forming and storing memories, as well as regulating mood and emotions. A smaller hippocampus may impair these functions, leading to difficulties in learning, memory, and emotional regulation, which are common symptoms of depression.

The hippocampus, a vital brain structure, plays a pivotal role in memory formation and learning processes. It acts as a key component of the brain's memory system, responsible for encoding, storing, and retrieving information. Additionally, the hippocampus is involved in spatial navigation, helping us form mental maps of our surroundings.

Studies suggest that patients with depression have a smaller hippocampus than those who do not have the illness. In one study, researchers used magnetic resonance imaging (MRI) to measure the size of the hippocampus in patients with depression and healthy controls. They found that the hippocampus was significantly smaller in depressed patients compared to the controls.

So, why does depression cause the hippocampus to shrink? The exact mechanisms are poorly understood, but there are several theories. One theory states that patients with depression have elevated stress hormone cortisol, which can damage the hippocampus over time. The body releases cortisol in response to stress, and chronic stress can lead to sustained elevation of cortisol levels. In addition, animal studies have shown that prolonged exposure to high levels of cortisol can cause damage to the hippocampus.

Another theory is that reduced hippocampal volume is a result of decreased neurogenesis – the formation of new neurons. Studies have shown that neurogenesis occurs in the hippocampus and is crucial for memory and mood regulation. In patients with depression, however, the rate of neurogenesis may be reduced, which could contribute to the smaller hippocampal volume.

Regardless of the exact mechanisms, the fact remains that depression can cause significant changes to the structure of the brain. This can have implications for treatment, as well as for the long-term outcome of the illness.

For example, antidepressant medication increases hippocampal volume in some patients, suggesting that treatment may be able to reverse some of the damages caused by depression.

References

1. https://www.bridgestorecovery.com/blog/depression-damage-and-regeneration-the-effects-of-hippocampal-atrophy/
2. https://www.theguardian.com/society/2015/jun/30/chronic-depression-shrinks-brains-memories-and-emotions#:~:text=The%20hippocampus%2C%20an%20area%20of,a%20global%20study%20has%20found.
3. https://www.healthline.com/health/depression-physical-effects-on-the-brain
4. https://www.ncbi.nlm.nih.gov/pmc/articles/PMC60045/

RELATIONSHIP BETWEEN FOOD AND HIPPOCAMPUS SIZE

When it comes to your brain health, you might not immediately think of food as a major factor. However, the food you eat can have a significant impact on various regions of your brain, including the hippocampus.

Several studies have suggested a link between the size of the hippocampus and dietary factors. Specifically, certain dietary patterns and nutrients influence hippocampal volume.

For example, research has found that a diet high in saturated fat and sugar can negatively impact hippocampal volume. In one study, participants who consumed a diet high in saturated fat had a smaller hippocampal volume than those who followed a healthier diet. Similarly, a diet high in added sugars was associated with a smaller hippocampal volume and poorer cognitive performance.

On the other hand, eating plenty of fruits and vegetables and other plant-based foods regularly has been linked to a larger hippocampal volume. A study suggests that older adults who consumed higher amounts of fruits and vegetables had a larger hippocampal volume and better memory performance.

Lastly, even caloric restriction may benefit the hippocampus. Some animal studies have demonstrated that restricting caloric intake can increase hippocampal neurogenesis (the growth of new neurons) and improve cognitive function. However, more research is required to determine if these findings apply to humans.

References

1. https://www.nature.com/articles/s41430-020-00734-z
2. https://www.ncbi.nlm.nih.gov/pmc/articles/PMC6237674/
3. https://bmcmedicine.biomedcentral.com/articles/10.1186/s12916-015-0461-x
4. https://time.com/5279288/how-diet-affects-your-brain-size/#:~:text=They%20also%20had%20more%20grey,people%20who%20ate%20healthier%20diets.

The Brain is Vibrant and Dynamic, an Organ of Connections

The brain is composed of billions of nerve cells, also known as neurons, which communicate with each other through a network of connections called synapses. These connections constantly form, strengthen, and weaken in response to your experiences and environment.

For example, suppose you learn a new skill or task, such as playing a musical instrument or speaking a new language. In that case, your brain forms new connections with neurons to encode that information. Over time, these connections become more robust and efficient, allowing you perform the task more efficiently and automatically.

Similarly, suppose you experience a traumatic event or suffer from chronic stress. In that case, your brain may adapt by forming new connections or strengthening existing ones in regions involved in emotional regulation and stress response.

Again, this can have both positive and negative effects on your mental and physical health, depending on the nature and the intensity of the stressor.

The brain is also capable of neuroplasticity, or the ability to change and reorganize in response to injury or disease. For example, suppose you suffer a stroke or traumatic brain injury. In that case, your brain may be able to rewire itself to compensate for the damage and regain lost function.

By understanding how the brain works and taking steps to support its health and function, you can optimize your mental and physical well-being and lead a more fulfilling life.

References

1. https://www.health.harvard.edu/blog/brain-plasticity-how-learning-changes-your-brain-201605249846
2. https://www.health.harvard.edu/blog/how-addiction-hijacks-the-brain-201603039338
3. https://faculty.washington.edu/chudler/introb.html
4. https://www.psychologytoday.com/us/blog/the-athletes-way/201705/what-is-neuroplasticity-and-why-is-it-so-important
5. https://www.scientificamerican.com/article/the-power-of-connection/
6. https://www.nimh.nih.gov/health/topics/neuroplasticity/index.shtml

The Role of Serotonin in Depression and Anxiety

Serotonin, or 5-hydroxytryptamine (5-HT), is a neurotransmitter that is crucial in regulating mood, behaviour, and emotional responses. However, in depression and anxiety, serotonin levels are often imbalanced, leading to a variety of symptoms.

In depression, the low levels of serotonin contribute to the development of the disorder. It regulates mood by modulating the activity of other neurotransmitters, including dopamine and norepinephrine. In depressed individuals, there is a reduction in the availability of serotonin in the brain, which can lead to decreased activity in these other neurotransmitter systems, ultimately leading to a decrease in mood and motivation.

Similarly, in anxiety disorders, it is believed that imbalances in serotonin levels contribute to the symptoms of the disorder. Since serotonin regulates stress response, its imbalances over-activate the stress response system, leading to feelings of anxiety and panic.

Studies have demonstrated that drugs that boost serotonin levels, for instance, selective serotonin reuptake inhibitors (SSRIs), can effectively treat both depression and anxiety. SSRIs function by obstructing the reabsorption of serotonin in the brain, which permits more serotonin to be present to regulate mood and anxiety.

However, the relationship between serotonin and Depression and anxiety is not straightforward, and there are likely to be many factors that contribute to the development of these disorders. While low serotonin levels implicate the development of depression and anxiety, it is also possible that imbalances in other neurotransmitters or other physiological factors play a role.

BDNF (BRAIN-DERIVED NEUROTROPHIC FACTOR) AND ITS ROLE

Even though the exact causes of depression are not fully understood, one important factor that contributes to the development and treatment of depression is a protein called brain-derived neurotrophic factor (BDNF).

The brain produces a protein named BDNF, which helps promote the growth and survival of neurons. It plays a key role in neuroplasticity, which is the ability of our brain to change and adapt in response to new experiences and learning.

BDNF is involved in many different aspects of brain function, including memory, learning, and mood regulation.

Researches suggest reduced BDNF levels in people with depression. In addition, individuals with depression have lower levels of BDNF in their blood and cerebrospinal fluid when compared to healthy individuals.

This has led researchers to investigate whether increasing BDNF levels could be a potential treatment for depression.

Inadditiontoitspotentialroleinthetreatmentofdepression, BDNF also implicates the development of depression. Animal studies have found that chronic stress, which is a known risk factor for depression, can lead to decreased levels of BDNF in the brain. This suggests that a lack of BDNF may be one of the ways in which chronic stress contributes to the development of depression.

There is also evidence to suggest that genetic factors may affect the relationship between BDNF and depression. Some studies have found that certain genetic variations that affect the formation of BDNF or function may have a link with an elevated risk of developing depression.

EFFECTS OF INFLAMMATION AND ROLE OF IMMUNITY

When it comes to Depression, many people tend to focus on the psychological aspects of the condition. However, research has shown that there is also a strong connection between Depression and inflammation in the body. The body's immune system also plays a crucial role in regulating the symptoms of Depression.

Research has shown that people with Depression often have elevated levels of inflammatory markers present in their blood, such as C-reactive protein (CRP), interleukin-6 (IL-6), and tumour necrosis factor-alpha (TNF-alpha). Produced by immune cells in response to inflammation, these markers have a link to multiple health problems, including heart disease, diabetes, and Alzheimer's disease.

So, how does inflammation contribute to Depression? One theory is that inflammation can disrupt the balance of neurotransmitters in the brain, which are responsible for regulating mood, sleep, and appetite. For example, inflammation can decrease serotonin levels, a neurotransmitter often targeted by antidepressant medications.

In addition, inflammation can also affect the structure and function of the brain itself. Research has shown that chronic inflammation can lead to a reduction in the volume of the hippocampus. This part of the brain is important for learning, memory, and emotion regulation. Inflammation can also lead to increased oxidative stress, which can damage neurons and contribute to cognitive decline.

So, how can you protect yourself against the adverse effects of inflammation on depression? A simple way is to adopt a healthy lifestyle, such as following a regular exercise regime, eating a balanced diet, and practising stress management techniques such as mindfulness meditation. These strategies can help reduce chronic inflammation and improve overall immune function.

Although depression is a complex condition with multiple contributing factors, inflammation and immune function play an important role in both its development and treatment.

WHAT HAPPENS IF INFLAMMATION CONTINUES FOR A LONG TIME: CHRONIC INFLAMMATION & ITS RELATIONSHIP WITH DEPRESSION & ANXIETY

If you have depression, it is possible that you may experience chronic inflammation in your body. Chronic inflammation occurs when your body's immune system remains active for extended periods, even when there is no apparent threat or injury.

When inflammation persists, it can have serious consequences for your physical and mental health. It worsens depression symptoms. Inflammation triggers the production of cytokines, which are proteins that act as messengers between cells in your body. These cytokines are capable of crossing the blood-brain barrier and affect the brain's chemistry, leading to changes in mood, motivation, and behaviour.

Studies have shown that people with depression who have higher levels of cytokines in their blood tend to have more severe symptoms and a poorer response to treatment. Inflammation may also reduce the effectiveness of antidepressant medications, making it more challenging to manage your depression.

Additionally, chronic inflammation may impair the functioning of the hippocampus. This part of the brain affects memory and learning. This impairment can make it more challenging to form new memories, concentrate, and make decisions, further complicating your ability to manage your depression.

HOW INFLAMMATION IMPACTS THE BRAIN

Inflammation is a natural immune response that occurs when your body is trying to protect itself from injury, infection, or disease. When inflammation occurs in your body, it can significantly impact your brain. However, when inflammation is chronic or excessive in nature, it can negatively affect the brain.

One of the main ways how inflammation impacts your brain is by disrupting the blood-brain barrier, a protective layer that surrounds your brain and prevents harmful substances from entering. When inflammation occurs, it can cause the blood-brain barrier to become more permeable, allowing toxins and other harmful substances to enter your brain. This can lead to inflammation in your brain, which can contribute to a variety of neurological conditions.

In addition to disrupting the blood-brain barrier, inflammation can also lead to changes in the structure and function of your brain cells. For instance, chronic inflammation can cause damage to your neurons, which are the cells responsible for transmitting signals throughout your brain. This damage can lead to cognitive impairment, memory problems, and other neurological symptoms.

Furthermore, inflammation can also disrupt the production of neurotransmitters, which are the chemicals that allow your neurons to communicate with each other. Disrupted neurotransmitter production can lead to imbalances in your brain chemistry, which can contribute to mood disorders such as depression and anxiety.

And lastly, inflammation can also impact the production of new brain cells, essential for learning, memory, and other cognitive functions. When inflammation occurs, it can inhibit the growth of new brain cells, leading to impaired brain function.

PROTECTION AGAINST INFLAMMATION IN BRAIN-ASTROCYTES, MICROGLIA

When it comes to protecting your brain from inflammation, it is important to understand the roles of two key players: astrocytes and microglia. These cells are responsible for maintaining the health and function of your brain. Still, when they become activated due to inflammation, they can contribute to further damage and dysfunction.

Here are some tips for protecting your brain against inflammation in these important cells:

- **Maintain a healthy diet:** Your brain needs a variety of nutrients to function properly, and eating brain-friendly foods can improve your brain health. Some specific nutrients that benefit the brain include omega-3 fatty acids, antioxidants like vitamins E and C, and polyphenols found in foods like blueberries and green tea.
- **Exercise regularly:** Exercising regularly has been shown to have numerous benefits for brain health, including reducing inflammation. Exercise can also promote the production of neurotrophic factors, which help support the growth and survival of neurons in the brain.
- **Consider supplements:** Some supplements, including curcumin (found in turmeric), resveratrol (found in grapes and red wine), and omega-3 fatty acids, have been shown to have anti-inflammatory effects on the brain.
- **Seek medical attention:** If you are positive for symptoms of inflammation in the brain, such as headaches, memory problems, or changes in mood or behaviour, it is essential to seek medical attention. Your healthcare provider can help determine the underlying cause(s) of your symptoms and recommend appropriate treatments.

By taking these steps to protect your brain against inflammation in astrocytes and microglia, you can help maintain optimal brain health and function.

WHY IS INFLAMMATION GOOD FOR THE BRAIN?

Inflammation is a complex biological response that occurs when the body's immune system is activated to protect against infection, injury, or other types of damage. While chronic inflammation can be harmful, acute inflammation plays an important role in the body's healing process, including the brain.

Researches show that inflammation in the brain has stimulated the growth of new brain cells and strengthened the connections between existing neurons, which can improve cognitive function and help repair damage caused by injury or disease. Inflammation can also help clear away harmful substances, such as plaques, that can build up in the brain and contribute to neurodegenerative disorders like Alzheimer's disease.

However, it's important to note that while inflammation can be beneficial for the brain in certain situations, chronic inflammation can have adverse effects on brain health and function. So, while inflammation is an important part of the body's natural healing process, it's essential to maintain a healthy balance to promote optimal brain function.

Anxiety is the fear of something imaginary- all threats and fears are imaginary until it is a threat to your physical existence.

Anxiety can be a crippling feeling that seems to consume you entirely. You may find yourself constantly worrying about what could go wrong or imagining all the worst-case scenarios in your head. The fear that you experience is often unwarranted, and it can be challenging to rationalize with yourself at the moment.

It is important to understand that all threats and fears are imaginary until they become a threat to your physical existence. This means that the anxiety that you are feeling is not necessarily based on reality but rather on the possibilities of what could happen. Your mind may be playing tricks on you, making you believe that things are worse than they actually are.

It is essential to recognize that anxiety is often based on irrational thoughts and beliefs. These thoughts can be difficult to control, and they can be overwhelming at times. However, it is essential to remember that these fears are often unfounded and not based on actual threats to your physical existence.

When you feel anxious, take a step back, assess your situation and act objectively. Ask yourself if there is a real threat to your physical safety or if it's just your mind playing tricks on you. You often experience fear in response to a perceived threat, even when the threat is not actually present.

It is also important to recognize that anxiety is manageable. There are techniques and strategies that you can use to reduce the impact of anxiety in your life. For example, mindfulness meditation, deep breathing exercises, and cognitive-behavioural therapy can all be effective tools in managing anxiety.

Remember, anxiety is not something that you have to live with forever. With the implementation of the right strategies and techniques, you can learn to manage your anxiety. So, the next time you feel overwhelmed by anxiety, take a deep inhale and remind yourself that all threats and fears are imaginary until they become a threat to your physical existence.

CAUSES OF BRAIN INFLAMMATION

The brain is the most vital and complex organ in the body. If you are experiencing brain inflammation, it can be a scary and overwhelming experience. Any inflammation affecting the brain can cause a range of symptoms and potentially serious health consequences. Understanding the possible causes of brain inflammation can help you take steps to protect your brain and promote healing.

Infection is the most common cause of brain inflammation- caused by viruses, bacteria, fungi, and other microorganisms that enter the body and affect the brain. Some common infections that can cause brain inflammation include meningitis, encephalitis, and Lyme disease. These infections can be serious and require prompt medical attention.

When the immune system mistakenly attacks the healthy cells and tissues in your body, it can cause inflammation in various organs, including the brain. Conditions such as multiple sclerosis, lupus, and sarcoidosis can all cause brain inflammation. Autoimmune disorders can also lead to brain inflammation.

Traumatic brain injuries (TBIs) are another potential cause of brain inflammation. When you experience a blow to the head, it can cause inflammation and swelling in the brain tissue, resulting in a wide range of symptoms, such as headaches, dizziness, confusion, and memory loss.

Certain medications can also lead to brain inflammation. For example, some antibiotics and anti-inflammatory drugs increase the risk of brain inflammation. If you're taking medication and experiencing symptoms of brain inflammation, it is important to talk to your doctor immediately.

Furthermore, many environmental factors can also cause brain inflammation. Exposure to toxins such as lead, mercury, and other heavy metals can cause inflammation in the brain. Additionally, air pollution and other environmental factors can also contribute to inflammation in the brain.

DIET'S ROLE IN THE CAUSE OF BRAIN INFLAMMATION

The food we eat has a direct impact on our body. Foods such as processed and fried foods, sugary drinks, and foods high in saturated fats are capable of causing inflammation in the body, especially the brain. This is because they trigger the release of pro-inflammatory chemicals, leading to chronic inflammation related to a broad range of health problems, including brain inflammation. If you do not have any ailment, you are surely doing something right in terms of diet, exercise and lifestyle.

In contrast, consuming foods rich in anti-inflammatory properties, like whole grains, nuts, fruits, vegetables, and fatty fish, decreases inflammation in the body and the brain. In addition, these foods contain vitamins, antioxidants, and minerals that can protect against inflammation and oxidative stress in the brain.

CELIAC DISEASE AND ITS RELATION WITH DEPRESSION AND ANXIETY

Celiac disease is an autoimmune disorder. It is a condition in which the body's immune system reacts to gluten. The ingestion of gluten can cause damage to the small intestine, leading to various symptoms, such as abdominal pain, bloating, and diarrhoea.

Recent studies have suggested that celiac disease has a link with depression and anxiety. One theory is that the inflammation caused by the immune system's response to gluten may trigger changes in the brain, leading to mood disorders.

In addition, people with celiac disease may also have lower levels of certain nutrients—for example, vitamin B12 and folate.

Research has shown that treating celiac disease with a gluten-free diet may improve mood and cognitive function in some individuals with celiac disease who also experience depression or anxiety. However, not all individuals with celiac disease will experience these mood disorders.

The food you consume affects the body's decisions to deploy your immune system.

Consuming a balanced diet that includes healthy foods promotes a healthy immune system and reduces the risk of illness. On the contrary, consuming a diet rich in processed foods, trans-fats, saturated fats, and sugars contributes to inflammation in the body and weakens the immune system. This makes it more difficult for the body to fight infections and illnesses.

In addition, some foods, such as those containing allergens or toxins, can trigger an immune response, leading to symptoms such as inflammation, rashes, and digestive issues.

DIET CAN ALSO ALLEVIATE INFLAMMATION

Inflammation is the body's response to foreign attacks in terms of infection, injury, toxins, heat, and others. Most people experience a combination of diseases today, where eating junk food has become more accessible than healthy meals.

Each ingredient you eat has an effect on controlling the inflammatory process in the body. Hence, carefully adding anti-inflammatory and anti-oxidant rich food items to the diet can help reduce inflammatory episodes. Many foods have anti-inflammatory properties that can benefit people with inflammatory issues. Some examples include water, mushrooms, ginger, omega-3 fatty acids, green tea, green leafy vegetables, and others.

INFLAMMATION-FIGHTING NUTRIENTS- OMEGA-3, MAGNESIUM, ETC.-- AND FOODS THAT HAVE THOSE NUTRIENTS

Several nutrients have anti-inflammatory properties, including:

1. **Omega-3 fatty acids:** These are present in fatty fish, such as salmon, sardines, and mackerel, as well as in plant-based sources, such as flaxseeds, chia seeds, and walnuts. Omega-3s lower inflammation in the body and prevent chronic diseases.

2. **Magnesium:** This mineral is present in leafy greens, nuts, seeds, and whole grains. It plays a role in more than 300 biochemical reactions in the body, including those that regulate inflammation. Studies show that magnesium supplements reduce inflammation in people with certain conditions, such as asthma and osteoporosis.
3. **Vitamin D:** Primarily obtained through exposure to sunlight, this nutrient is also present in fatty fish, egg yolks, and fortified foods. Vitamin D regulates immune function and helps regulate inflammation in the body.
4. **Antioxidants:** These include vitamins A, C, and E, as well as selenium and zinc. They are found in fruits, vegetables, nuts, and seeds and help protect the body against oxidative stress, which can contribute to inflammation.
5. **Probiotics:** These are "good" bacteria found in fermented foods, such as yoghurt, dhokla, dosas, kefir, kimchi, kombucha, miso, and sauerkraut. They help support a healthy gut microbiomes, which reduce inflammation in the body.

The brain is a dynamic organ that can always change; you have the power to change it.

The brain is a dynamic and adaptable organ that has the ability to change throughout a person's life. This is known as neuroplasticity. This quality allows the brain to adapt to new experiences, learn new skills, and recover from injury.

Researches have shown that certain activities such as exercise, meditation, and learning new things, can promote neuroplasticity and help improve brain function.

For example, regular exercise increases the production of growth factors in the brain, which can help promote the growth of new neurons and synapses.

In addition, engaging in activities that challenge the brain, such as learning a new language or playing an instrument, can also promote neuroplasticity and improve cognitive function.

Therefore, engaging in activities that promote neuroplasticity and making healthy lifestyle choices help promote the health and function of your brain and improve your overall well-being.

RELATIONSHIP BETWEEN INTESTINES AND MENTAL HEALTH

The relationship between the intestines and mental health is a fascinating topic that has garnered significant attention recently. It is now a widely accepted fact that there exists a connection between our guts' and brains' health. This relationship is known as the gut-brain axis, a complex communication network between the intestines and the brain.

Our gut plays an important role in regulating neurotransmitters and other neurochemicals that are crucial for our mental well-being. You may have experienced this yourself when you've had a "gut feeling" or "butterflies in the abdomen" during a stressful situation. This is because the gut contains millions of nerve cells, known as the enteric nervous system, that communicate with the brain.

The gut-brain axis is the communication centre between the intestines and brain about food intake. Our brain needs to know whether we've eaten enough to feel satiated when we eat. This communication between the intestines and the brain is crucial for maintaining a healthy weight and avoiding overeating.

However, this communication can also go awry. For example, if we eat something that is harmful to our system, such as toxins or pathogens, our brain will respond by inducing vomiting or diarrhoea to expel the harmful substance.

The microbiome, a collection of microorganisms that live in our gut, plays an essential role in regulating the gut-brain axis. These microorganisms send signals to the brain through the enteric nervous system, which can impact our mental well-being.

Probiotics, or beneficial bacteria that we consume through certain foods or supplements can help maintain a healthy microbiome. The microbiome is crucial for the digestion and absorption of nutrients; without it, we would not be able to extract the necessary nutrients from our food.

Studies have demonstrated that people with a healthy microbiome are better able to cope with stress. In contrast, those with an unhealthy microbiome are more likely to experience anxiety and depression. There is also a link between the bacteria in our gut and our stress response.

So, how exactly do the "good bugs" in our intestines work on the brain? One way is through the production of neurotransmitters. Interestingly, the majority of serotonin neurons are present in the intestines, not the brain.

Another way that the gut communicates with the brain is through the vagus nerve, which is the third mode of communication in the gut-brain axis. The vagus nerve is involved in modulating hunger and stress and regulating the immune response.

In conclusion, a healthy gut is essential for a healthy brain. The gut-brain axis is a complex and fascinating network of communication that impacts many aspects of our mental and physical well-being. By taking care of our gut through proper nutrition, exercise, and stress management, we can help maintain a healthy microbiome and support our mental health.

PROBIOTICS TREATMENT AND ITS LINK WITH BIPOLAR DISORDER

Bipolar disorder is a mental health disorder. It affects an individual's mood, energy, activity levels, and ability to function in daily life. The symptoms can be challenging to manage, and treatment modalities vary depending on the severity of the condition. In recent years, probiotics have emerged as a potential treatment option for bipolar disorder, and many researchers have investigated the link between probiotics and this mental health condition.

The human body contains trillions of good and bad bacteria, and probiotics help maintain a balance of healthy bacteria in the gut. Probiotics are healthy and alive bacteria and yeasts benefit our health, specifically the digestive system. They are often present in fermented foods such as yoghurt, kefir, and sauerkraut and consumed as supplements.

Researches have demonstrated a link between gut health and mental health. The gut contains millions of neurons. It is also considered the second brain. Studies have found that the gut microbiome can impact brain function and behaviour and link imbalances in the gut microbiome with several mental health conditions, including depression and anxiety.

PROBIOTICS CAN HELP IN REDUCING INTESTINAL INFLAMMATION

The gut is a complex ecosystem comprising many microorganisms, including bacteria, viruses, fungi, and protozoa. The gut microbiota is crucial in maintaining intestinal homeostasis and overall health. However, certain factors such as diet, lifestyle, medications, and stress can disrupt the balance of the gut microbiota, leading to dysbiosis, inflammation, and other health problems.

Probiotics are good live bacteria that confer health benefits when administered in adequate amounts. They are found naturally in certain foods, such as yoghurt and fermented vegetables, or consumed as dietary supplements.

Studies show that probiotics can potentially prevent and treat various health problems, including gastrointestinal disorders, allergies, and infections. In recent years, the use of probiotics to reduce intestinal inflammation has been of keen interest.

Let's discuss the scientific evidence that supports the use of probiotics to lower intestinal inflammation. Let us start with understanding the mechanisms by which probiotics exert their anti-inflammatory effects, followed by a review of the research on the use of probiotics for various inflammatory bowel diseases and other intestinal inflammatory conditions.

MECHANISMS OF ACTION OF PROBIOTICS IN REDUCING INTESTINAL INFLAMMATION

The exact mechanism by which probiotics implement their anti-inflammatory effects has yet to be fully understood. However, several mechanisms have been proposed based on experimental and clinical evidences.

- Immunomodulation
- Barrier function
- Microbial interactions

EVIDENCE FOR THE USE OF PROBIOTICS IN INFLAMMATORY BOWEL DISEASES

Inflammatory bowel diseases (IBD) are chronic inflammatory disorders of the gastrointestinal tract. The exact cause of IBD is not known. Still, the belief is that it occurs from a combination of genetic, environmental, and immunological factors.

Several clinical trials have investigated the use of probiotics in the treatment of IBD. A systematic review and a meta-analysis of randomised controlled trials found that probiotics can improve clinical remission rates in patients with mild-to-moderate ulcerative colitis but not in those with Crohn's disease.

EVIDENCE FOR THE USE OF PROBIOTICS IN OTHER INTESTINAL INFLAMMATORY CONDITIONS

Probiotics can also potentially reduce inflammation in other intestinal conditions, including infectious diarrhoea, irritable bowel syndrome (IBS), and celiac disease.

Higher doses of probiotic supplementation can also lead to gas, bloating, and even brain fog; that's why figuring out the right amount of probiotic supplementation is tricky.

Probiotics are living microorganisms. They provide health benefits to the host when consumed in adequate quantities. The popularity of probiotic supplements has grown in recent decades due to the growing interest in gut health and the microbiome.

Probiotics can play a crucial role in maintaining a healthy gut microbiome, which may promote overall health and well-being. However, like any supplement, probiotics have their drawbacks. One of the most significant challenges regarding probiotic supplementation is determining the correct dosage. Higher doses of probiotics can lead to gas, bloating, and brain fog, among other adverse effects.

PROBIOTICS AND THE GUT MICROBIOME

The gut microbiome is essential intestinal microorganisms that reside in the gut, primarily in the large intestine. These microorganisms are vital in various physiological functions, such as digestion, immunity, and metabolism. The gut microbiome contains both beneficial and harmful bacteria, and the balance between the two is critical for maintaining a healthy gut.

Probiotics also play a significant role in maintaining a healthy gut microbiome. They are living microorganisms that, when ingested in sufficient quantities, can provide health benefits to the host. Probiotics work by altering the composition of the gut microbiome, increasing the number of beneficial bacteria and decreasing the number of harmful bacteria.

DETERMINING THE RIGHT DOSAGE OF PROBIOTICS

One of the most challenging aspects of probiotic supplementation is determining the right dosage. The number of probiotics needed to provide health benefits can vary depending on factors such as age, sex, health status, and the specific strain of bacteria.

There is no universally recommended dosage for probiotics, and the amount needed to yield health benefits varies depending on the individual and the particular bacterial strain.

Most probiotic supplements contain between 1 billion and 10 billion colony-forming units (CFUs) per dose. However, some supplements may contain up to 100 billion CFUs per dose.

ADVERSE EFFECTS OF HIGHER DOSES OF PROBIOTICS

While probiotics are generally considered safe, higher doses of probiotics can lead to adverse effects. Some of the most common adverse effects of higher doses of probiotics include gas, bloating, and brain fog.

Gas and Bloating: Gas and bloating are common issues of probiotic supplementation. Probiotics produce gas as they ferment undigested carbohydrates in the gut. This gas can lead to bloating, discomfort, and flatulence.

Brain Fog: Consumption of higher doses of probiotics can lead to an adverse effect known as brain fog. This term refers to a sense of mental fatigue, difficulty in concentrating, and confusion. The exact cause of brain fog is not completely clear. Still, it may be connected to the production of neurotoxins by specific bacterial strains.

Other Adverse Effects: Other adverse effects of higher doses of probiotics include diarrhoea, constipation, and abdominal pain. These side effects are mild and resolve by themselves within a few days. However, in rare cases, probiotics can lead to more severe adverse effects, such as infections in people with weakened immune systems.

The best way to influence the microbiome is through making changes in diet. Diet changes will also provide fibre content for healthy bacteria to thrive. A Mediterranean diet with fermented food can greatly help the brain. Fruits and vegetables can also provide fibre, which is good for the intestines.

The microorganisms in the human gut consist of bacteria, viruses, fungi, and archaea. They are together known as the gut microbiome. This microbiome is crucial for preserving human health. It has associations with various conditions such as mental health disorders, inflammatory bowel disease, obesity, and type 2 diabetes.

Modifying the diet is one of the most efficient methods to impact the gut microbiome. Diet can greatly influence the composition and variety of microorganisms present in the gut, which in turn can impact overall health.

The subsequent sections will examine the link between diet, the gut microbiome, and human health and suggest dietary changes that can promote a healthy gut microbiome.

THE MEDITERRANEAN DIET AND FERMENTED FOODS

The Mediterranean diet emphasises whole foods, such as fruits, vegetables, whole grains, legumes, nuts, and seeds, and healthy fats, like olive oil and fatty fish. The Mediterranean diet is also rich in fermented foods like yoghurt, kefir, sauerkraut, and kimchi.

Foods exposed to microorganisms like bacteria, yeasts, and fungi are called fermented foods. This process can enhance the taste and texture of food, increase the availability of nutrients, and create helpful bacteria that can aid in gut health.

The Mediterranean diet is full of fibre. This serves as a food source for healthy gut bacteria and contains polyphenols, which are plant-based substances that possess anti-inflammatory and antioxidant properties.

Fermented foods like kefir and yoghurt are probiotics, which are living microorganisms that offer health advantages when ingested in sufficient quantities. Probiotics can help enhance gut health by lowering inflammation, promoting intestinal barrier function, and regulating the immune system.

In addition to fermented foods, the Mediterranean diet is rich in prebiotic foods, promoting the growth and activity of beneficial gut bacteria. Prebiotic foods include onions, garlic, leeks, asparagus, and Jerusalem artichokes.

THE IMPORTANCE OF FRUITS AND VEGETABLES

Fruits and vegetables are rich in nutrients, fibre, and phytochemicals. Phytochemicals are plant-based compounds with antioxidant and anti-inflammatory properties and can promote gut health.

Some fruits and vegetables are high in resistant starch, which is a type of dietary fibre that controls digestion in the small intestine. It also ferments in the large intestine. Resistant starch can increase the production of short-chain fatty acids, which are beneficial compounds that can reduce inflammation and promote gut health.

Look at your plate next time you have a meal. Does your plate look full of fibre, greens, veggies, beans, nuts, whole grains, and fermented food?

TYPES OF FERMENTED FOODS

As we have already established, it is highly important to eat a meal that consists of a variety of nutrients in proportions that your body needs. This means you must ensure you have enough fibre, greens and vegetables to ensure smooth digestion and excretion.

Furthermore, there should be enough proteins to give you the energy to get through your day. Eating whole grains and fermented foods brings their own set of benefits. Some of the most beneficial types of fermentation include:

- Lactic acid fermentation involves yeast strains and bacteria that convert starches or sugars into lactic acid. Lactic acid fermentation does not require heat for its preparation.
- Ethanol fermentation: This type is also known as alcohol fermentation.
- Acetic acid fermentation

Add these foods to your meals and give a boost to your health.

FOODS TO KNOCKOUT DEPRESSION

We see food as a means of satisfying hunger. Still, it can also be a powerful tool for maintaining good mental health. Depression and anxiety can significantly affect a person's well-being and make it difficult to perform daily tasks. While medication and therapy are commonly used treatments for these conditions, a balanced diet can also play an important role in preventing or alleviating symptoms.

GREEN LEAFY VEGETABLES

Green leafy vegetables are an excellent source of nutrients that can help support brain health. They have vitamins and minerals, like folate, magnesium, and vitamin K, which are important for cognitive function.

Additionally, they are high in phytonutrients, such as lutein and zeaxanthin. They improve mood and prevent cognitive decline.

RED AND PURPLE LEAFY VEGETABLES

Red and purple leafy vegetables also offer a range of brain-boosting nutrients. These vegetables contain anthocyanins, powerful antioxidants that protect the brain from oxidative stress. They also contain vitamin C, which is important for mood regulation and immune function.

EIGHT COLORS OF FOOD

Eating a variety of colourful foods is important for overall health and well-being. Each colour represents different phytonutrients, which can help support different health aspects. For example, orange foods, such as sweet potatoes and carrots, contain beta-carotene, which is important for eye health and immune function.

Eating various colourful foods can also help prevent or alleviate depression and anxiety. For example, blue and purple foods, such as blueberries and blackberries, contain anthocyanins, which improve mood and cognitive function.

NUTS, SEEDS, AND BEANS

Nuts, seeds, and beans are rich in protein, healthy fats, and fibre, making them highly beneficial for brain health. They also provide a host of essential minerals and vitamins like magnesium and zinc, essential for maintaining brain functions. Furthermore, these foods are rich in phytonutrients, such as flavonoids, linked with enhanced cognitive function and reduced risk of depression.

Almonds, chia seeds, and black beans are a few examples of nuts, seeds, and beans you can easily incorporate into your diet. Add these foods to your smoothies and salads, or consume them as a snack.

MEATS AND SEAFOOD

Meats and seafood are also important sources of protein and nutrients that can support brain health. Fish, in particular, contains omega-3 fatty acids, which are important for cognitive function and mood regulation.

Additionally, meats and seafood are high in vitamin B12, which is essential for brain function and the production of neurotransmitters.

Some examples of meats and seafood include salmon, tuna, and lean beef. There are various ways to cook these foods, such as by grilling or baking.

EGGS

Eggs are an excellent source of protein and nutrients that can support brain health. They contain choline, which is essential for cognitive function and memory. Also, eggs are high in vitamin D, improving mood and preventing depression.

DARK CHOCOLATE

Dark chocolate is a delicious treat that also offers a range of health benefits. It has flavonoids that improve cognitive function and mood. Additionally, dark chocolate contains small amounts of caffeine, which can enhance focus and concentration.

When choosing dark chocolate, look for options containing at least 70% cocoa to ensure you get the most health benefits.

BARRIERS TO CHANGING THE DIET

You may have heard the phrase, "You are what you eat," and this couldn't be true when it comes to your mental health. Studies suggest a strong link between what you eat and your mood, with certain foods exacerbating or relieving symptoms of depression.

While making dietary changes may seem a simple solution to improve your mental health, it is often easier said than done. Let us discuss some barriers that can prevent people with depression from changing their diets.

- Lack of knowledge and resources
- Comfort and emotional eating
- Lack of motivation and energy
- Social isolation and stigma
- Addiction to processed foods
- Fear of change

So, what can we do to overcome these barriers? Here are some options:

- Seek professional help
- Start small
- Build a support network
- Address emotional eating
- Educate yourself
- Make healthy options convenient
- Address addiction to processed foods

In conclusion, making dietary changes can be challenging, particularly for individuals with depression. However, the benefits of making these changes can significantly improve mental health and well-being.

By addressing the barriers to dietary change, seeking professional help, starting small, building a support network, addressing emotional eating, educating oneself, making healthy options convenient, and addressing addiction to processed foods, individuals with depression can make positive changes to their diet and improve their overall health and well-being.

COMMON QUESTIONS REGARDING CHANGING THE DIET

Depression, as we already established, is a complex mental health condition that requires significant effort to come out of. Even though it is treatable, with medications and therapies, we often overlook the importance of diet.

However, recent researches have shown that diet can play a significant role in depression management. If you're considering changing your diet to manage depression, we have answered some questions that you may have:

CAN CHANGING MY DIET REALLY HELP WITH DEPRESSION?

Yes, changing your diet can help with depression. Evidence suggests a link between diet and mental health, and many studies have shown that dietary changes can have a positive effect on depression.

Studies show that diets high in processed foods, saturated fats, and sugars are associated with an increased risk of depression. In contrast, diets associated with a lower risk of depression are rich in essential brain nutrients.

In particular, some studies have found that diets full of omega-3 fatty acids can have a positive effect on depression. Additionally, foods that contain probiotics, such as yoghurt and fermented foods, may also have a positive impact on mental health.

While changing your diet alone may not be a complete solution for depression, it can be a helpful complement to other treatments such as therapy and medication.

WHAT SPECIFIC FOODS SHOULD I EAT TO HELP MANAGE MY DEPRESSION?

While there is no specific food that can cure depression, there are certain foods that help manage symptoms. Some of these foods include:

- **Omega-3-rich fatty fish:** Salmon, tuna, and sardines are examples of fatty fish that contain high levels of omega-3 fatty acids, associated with reducing the risk of depression.
- **Folate-rich leafy greens:** Spinach, kale, and Swiss chard are leafy greens that are rich in folate, a nutrient linked to reducing the risk of depression.
- **Fibre-rich whole grains:** Brown rice, quinoa, and oats are examples of whole grains that are high in fibre, a nutrient linked to reducing the risk of depression.
- **Antioxidant-rich berries:** Blueberries, raspberries, and strawberries are types of berries that are high in antioxidants linked to reducing the risk of depression.
- **Magnesium-rich nuts and seeds:** Almonds, cashews, and pumpkin seeds are nuts and seeds that are high in magnesium, a nutrient linked to reducing the risk of depression.

ARE THERE ANY FOODS I SHOULD AVOID IF I HAVE DEPRESSION?

While there are no specific foods you should avoid, it is essential to limit your intake of processed foods, sugar, and unhealthy fats. These foods have a great link with an increased risk of depression.

CAN SUPPLEMENTS HELP WITH DEPRESSION?

While supplements can be helpful in managing depression, they cannot substitute for a healthy diet. Some supplements that may help manage depression symptoms include:

- **Omega-3 fatty acids:** Omega-3 supplements can be helpful in managing depression symptoms.
- **Vitamin D:** Vitamin D supplements can be helpful in managing depression symptoms, especially for people who are deficient in vitamin D.
- **B vitamins:** B vitamins can be helpful in managing depression symptoms, especially for people who are deficient in B vitamins.

SHOULD A HEALTHCARE PROFESSIONAL BE CONSULTED BEFORE CHANGING MY DIET FOR DEPRESSION?

Yes, it is essential to consult with a healthcare professional before making any dietary changes for Depression. A healthcare professional can help you develop a personalised plan that takes into account your specific nutritional needs and medical history. They can also monitor your progress and make any necessary adjustments to your plan.

CAN EXERCISE HELP MANAGE DEPRESSION?

Yes, exercise can be helpful in managing depression symptoms. Frequent Exercising releases endorphins, which are natural mood boosters. It also helps to reduce stress and anxiety, which can contribute to Depression.

CAN I STILL EAT MY FAVOURITE FOODS IF I HAVE DEPRESSION?

Yes, you can still eat your favourite foods if you have Depression. While dietary changes may be helpful in managing symptoms of Depression, it is not necessary to completely eliminate all of your favourite foods.

Maintaining a balanced and nutritious diet is essential, but it is possible to achieve this while still enjoying your favourite foods in moderation. It is also necessary to be mindful of how certain foods may affect your mood and energy levels. For example, while indulging in a piece of cake may bring you temporary pleasure, consuming too much sugar may lead to a subsequent crash in energy and mood.

Suppose you are concerned about how your diet may be affecting your mental health. In that case, speaking with a healthcare professional or registered dietitian is always a good idea. It's essential to keep in mind that managing depression often involves a multifaceted approach that includes therapy, medication, exercise, and lifestyle changes.

HOW TO MAKE A FOOD JOURNAL

Making a food diary is the easiest way to manage our emotions and to keep track of what we eat, when, why, and how frequently. By tracking these things, we become more obedient and honest toward self-improvement.

You can make a food diary based on your needs and add information about whatever you intend to track. If you are recovering from depression, maintaining a diary is a great way to monitor your food intake and moods when you eat a particular delicacy.

For example, you eat lunch at 1 pm and decide to watch your favourite series on Netflix, say, an emotional movie. While watching, you feel sad and decide to eat samosas and popcorn around 3 pm to change your mood. The samosas and popcorn are nothing but additional, unwanted foods that you rely upon for satiety. Here, you are trying to feel better by bingeing on foods which you otherwise wouldn't.

When you go through your food journal, you'll realise that your emotions pulled you into overeating. And henceforth, you can make a conscious effort to avoid doing this and take a step towards self-improvement.

Now that we've understood how the food journal would help us, let us understand what should be a part of our journal to help on our journey to recover from depression.

Some important aspects you may learn while making the food diary and keeping track of your habits have been discussed below.

WHAT IS YOUR DIET PATTERN?

Writing every time you eat in terms of what you eat, how much and how you felt at that time gives an idea about your diet pattern, which will help you associate other ongoing symptoms such as bloating, acidity, weight gain/loss, and others, if any.

YOUR RELATIONSHIP WITH YOU

Our food habits and moods often show us the mirror. They replicate how we feel about ourselves. For example, when we bite our nails or eat hastily, it is because we are anxious.

On the other hand, if you meet others happily and eat slowly, savouring every bite of your morsel, it implies you're in a good space.

YOUR RELATIONSHIP WITH FOOD

Our relationship with food often equates to the status of our mental health and mood. You may have noticed eating too little when you are disappointed or when someone hurts you.

Another example could be you relying on junk food or takeaways just to make yourself feel elated. These behaviours define your relationship with food.

HOW TO KEEP YOURSELF MOTIVATED?

It is not easy for us to handle our emotions and keep ourselves motivated to improve and do well in life. It's just not easy. However, there are a few tricks you could apply to fix your life like Bob the Builder fixes buildings. Here they are:

- **Set goals:** Stay motivated by setting specific and measurable goals. Track your progress by breaking your larger goals into small and achievable steps. Celebrate your accomplishments as you reach each milestone.

- **Change your diet plan:** Changing your diet can positively impact your energy levels and health. Consider working with a dietitian to create a healthy, balanced meal plan that meets your nutritional needs and fits your lifestyle.
- **Record your sleep pattern:** It is crucial for your overall physical and mental health to obtain adequate and high-quality sleep. Use a sleep tracking app or journal to record your sleep patterns, and aim to establish a consistent sleep schedule and bedtime routine.
- **Take your responsibilities:** Taking responsibility for your actions and choices can help you feel more in control of your life. Make a list of your responsibilities and prioritise them based on importance and urgency.
- **Record your fun activities:** Engaging in enjoyable activities can boost your mood and help you feel more motivated. Keep a list of activities you enjoy and make time for them regularly.
- **Innovate or do something new:** Trying new things can be exciting and help you stay motivated. Challenge yourself to learn a new skill or hobby or take on a new project at work or home.
- **Check your improvement:** Tracking your progress and checking your improvement can help you stay motivated. Use a journal or app to record your progress and, celebrate your successes, and use setbacks as learning opportunities to adjust your approach.

References

1 https://www.mensjournal.com/.amp/health-fitness/how-to-use-food-to-fight-depression-and-boost-mood-mens-journal

2 https://www.webmd.com/depression/features/writing-your-way-out-of-depression

3 https://www.healthline.com/nutrition/food-journaling-instructions-and-tips

4 https://www.healthyplace.com/self-help/food-mental-health/use-food-and-mood-diary-improve-your-mental-health

5 https://www.ncbi.nlm.nih.gov/pmc/articles/PMC6147775/

Other books by the Author

1. Decoding Obesity

This book is your essential guide to understanding and conquering obesity. This book provides insightful exploration and unveils the complexities of obesity, empowering you to take control of your health journey. Discover the hidden truths behind weight gain, debunk common myths, and embark on a transformative path to wellness. With expert advice on nutrition, lifestyle, and holistic health, this book is your key to unlocking a healthier, happier you. Don't miss out on the opportunity to decode the mysteries of obesity and embrace a vibrant future!

2. Irresistible Detox Elixirs: A Love Affair with Healthful Drinks

"Irresistible Detox Elixir" is your gateway to rejuvenation through delicious, health-boosting smoothies. This book is your sanctuary in a hectic world, offering vibrant recipes that cleanse, nourish, and energise. Each elixir is a blend of flavours and nutrients designed to elevate your well-being. Begin your journey to a revitalised, irresistible you today!

3. Vitamins & Minerals

Unlock vibrant health with the essential guide to vitamins and minerals! Explore their benefits, rich food sources, daily recommendations, and expert insights on managing deficiencies and avoiding excesses.

4. Arthritis is reversible

Shatter the Myths, Embrace Hope: Your Guide to a Brighter Future with Reversible Arthritis

Unmask the misconceptions and discover natural solutions for managing and potentially reversing arthritis.

5. Detox Your Body (free E-book, available on author's website)

Unveil your body's natural potential! Detox to eliminate toxins, discover the signs and benefits and explore a range of safe and effective methods for lasting transformation.

Embrace a vibrant you. Learn why detox matters, identify the need, unlock amazing benefits, and delve into practical internal cleansing and revitalisation strategies.

www.ingramcontent.com/pod-product-compliance
Ingram Content Group UK Ltd.
Pitfield, Milton Keynes, MK11 3LW, UK
UKHW020050200726
13845UKWH00055B/615